Help Club for Moms

Moms encouraging moms to know the love of Christ

The Wise Woman Loves

Hello Mom!

What a blessing you are to those around you! You may not realize it, but you are the vessel through which God's love is poured out to countless others. As women, our heart's desire is to love and be loved in return. In *The Wise Woman Loves* devotional workbook, we will uncover the truth surrounding God's unending, soul-quenching love for us, as well as His desire to mold us into women who love others in His capacity and strength. He alone is all we need on this journey as wives and mothers! He will meet us where we are and transform us, His precious daughters, into women who truly love well.

Are you ready to begin? Great, so are we! Through this study, we want to challenge you to commit **20 Minutes a Day to a Christ-Centered Home.**

Five Minutes of Prayer: Start your time with the Lord by seeking Him in prayer! Praise God for who He is (His kindness, goodness, grace, love, etc.), take a moment to thank Him for any blessings that come to your mind, and ask Him to speak to your heart as you read the day's devotion. We also encourage you to find a prayer partner to pray with over the phone for ten minutes each week. Praying with another godly woman will change your life!

Ten Minutes in God's Word and *The Wise Woman Loves Study*: Read the day's devotional, being sure to refer to all Scriptures mentioned. There are only three devotions each week, so feel free to spread each one out over two days, or dig deeper into the chapter where the Scriptures are found on days that you do not have a study. We want even the busiest mom to be able to spend time in the Bible with Jesus! Make sure to use the journaling lines to jot down what God has taught you through your time with Him today. Make note of Scriptures or thoughts that stood out to you or write down how you plan to implement the "Faith-Filled" ideas or *Help Club for Kids* discipleship tools mentioned in this book.

Five Minutes to Prepare for Your Day: Before you hit the ground running, take five minutes to plan your day. Write down your "Six Most Important List" which is simply six things you desire to accomplish that day. This list can include many things: perhaps a Mom Tip you would like to do (be sure to refer to the Mom Tips section each week!), a way you hope to encourage your husband or child that day, the meals you plan to prepare, or a task that needs to be finished in your home. Being intentional will make all the difference in both your impact on your family and the wellbeing of your home!

Well, that's it! Our whole team is praying for you to encounter Jesus, and grow in spiritual wisdom and understanding as you actively participate in our devotional workbook—*The Wise Woman Loves*.

Blessings and love,
The Help Club for Moms Team

P.S. – We would LOVE to bless you for buying this book by gifting several exclusive FREE printables to you. Thank you so much for supporting Help Club for Moms; we are so very blessed by you! **Check out myhelpclubformoms.com to access these printables.**

The Wise Woman Loves

The Wise Woman Loves

Homemaking

~ Week One ~

"Love never fails. But where there are prophecies,
they will cease; where there are tongues, they will be
stilled; where there is knowledge, it will pass away."

~ 1 Corinthians 13:8

Hello, Help Club Mamas!

Homemaking does not often come easily, but nothing of value ever does. What you are doing each day is not busywork; it's eternal investment. The secret to having our efforts stand the test of time is to do everything through God's love. In fact, the only homemaking that matters is that done in love, not perfection, because, "Love never fails. But where there are prophecies, they will cease; where there are tongues, they will be stilled; where there is knowledge, it will pass away" (1 Corinthians 13:8).

First on your checklist every morning before the laundry, the breakfast, or the rest, is to meet with Jesus. He wants to pour His love into you, and show you what really matters for the day. He will give you your marching orders! Take a deep breath—it will all get done eventually. One day your little mess makers will be gone, but your efforts will last.

God has given you everything you need to be the very homemaker your family needs. You have eyes that see the need and hands that work until it's done. You have a vision to train and a heart that disciples. You have a talent to bring beauty to each room and warmth for a soft landing. You have a humility that lets go of self, and a confidence which does not bother to compare. You have a faith that says "no way" to fear and knees that know when it's time to kneel. You have a sound mind to make it all work and a determination to do it all again. Be certain in your heart that He sees it all—every crumb swept, face washed, toy bin put back together, and every candle lit. He is especially pleased when you do it all for Him.

Mother, you are the beautifier of your home and the very fragrance of Christ's love in which your family may continually indulge. May I challenge you to recognize that the day-in and day-out duties of wife, mother, teacher, and keeper are not only benefiting your family, but they are also making you into the woman God destined you to be? As you faithfully serve and beautify, you are being refined—chiseled into the very image of love.

Love and Blessings,
Tara Fox and the Help Club for Moms Team

❝ *This job has been given to me to do. Therefore, it is a gift. Therefore, it is a privilege. Therefore, it is an offering I may make to God. Therefore, it is to be done gladly, if it is done for Him. Here, not somewhere else, I may learn God's way. In this job, not in some other, God looks for faithfulness.* **❞**

~ Elisabeth Elliot

Mom Tips

By: Leslie Leonard

"She watches over the ways of her household, and does not eat the bread of idleness." ~ Proverbs 31:27 (NET Bible)

The Wise Woman Builds Her Spirit

- Get a pad of spiral bound index cards to keep at your kitchen sink and download a voice recording app on your phone. These tools will be used frequently to help you memorize Scripture.
- Write 1 Timothy 5:14 on your notecards or in dry erase marker on your bathroom mirror or record it on your phone, and memorize the verse by the end of the week.

The Wise Woman Loves Her Husband

- Take back your master bedroom this week. Create a space of calm and relaxation for the two of you. Clear any piles of clutter, and put away that laundry that seems to pile up in the master bedroom. Spend an extra moment dusting and cleaning the window covering.
- Ask your husband how you can pray for him this week. Is he experiencing challenges at work that, by committing to pray, you can help ease the burden? Remember to listen with an open heart when he shares his burdens with you.

The Wise Woman Loves Her Children

- Spend a moment this week helping your children learn a new household task. Even young children can learn to vacuum, empty the dishwasher, and help with the laundry. Take Proverbs 22:6 to heart.
- Take time to read with your children this week. Commit to being present in the moment and turn off the smartphone during reading time.

The Wise Woman Cares For Her Home

- Plan what you are going to have for dinner by 9 a.m. every day this week. Try to utilize items you already have on hand to prepare family meals. Challenge yourself to think outside your regular meal rotation and use what is on your pantry shelves.
- Before you head to bed, take a moment to wipe down your kitchen counters and sink area. Do this small task every night this week. You will find you are more productive if you start the day with a clean kitchen.

> By wisdom a house is built, and through understanding it is established; through knowledge its rooms are filled with rare and beautiful treasures.
>
> ~ Proverbs 24:3-4

"What you do in your house is worth as much as if you did it up in heaven for our Lord God. We should accustom ourselves to think of our position and work as sacred and well-pleasing to God, not on account of the position and work, but on account of the word and faith from which the obedience and the work flow."
~ Martin Luther

- A big component of the Help Club for Moms is praying weekly with a prayer partner for 10 minutes. If you do not have anyone to pray with, ask God to bring her to you. He is faithful and will provide! This tiny habit of praying with a friend regularly will truly change your life!

- Dear mama, the Lord sees you! He sees your tired eyes and knows your heart's desires. Take the time to submit to Him today. Hide away in a quiet spot with a snack (chocolate, anyone?), your Bible, and your journal.

- Please read Proverbs 24:3-4. Write both verses in your journal. Pray and meditate on them for a few minutes before continuing to read.

Spirit-Filled Homemaking

By: Rachel Jones

Homemaking is so much more than cleaning a house, cooking food, and making sure your family has clothes to wear. Homemaking is about nurturing a spirit of warmth, comfort, and love in your home, as Proverbs says, "She looks well to the ways of her household and does not eat the bread of idleness" (Proverbs 31:27 ESV).

Whether you work outside the home or stay home full time, you are a homemaker. You have been called by God to make the place where you and your family live a home. Making your house a home is hard work, and I am currently in the trenches with you, ladies! I am home full-time with four kiddos under the age of nine, and my days are mostly spent in the kitchen and laundry room. What brings me comfort and fills my heart with peace and contentment is the Holy Spirit. Without His presence, I would be floundering without purpose or direction.

One of my favorite Bible verses is 2 Timothy 1:7 (NIV 1984), "For God did not give us a spirit of timidity, but a spirit of *power*, of love, and of *self-discipline*." You are all talented women of God who have the *power* to do what is right for your home. You have unconditional *love* from the Holy Spirit to care for your family. And within all of you is the *self-discipline* to keep your heart and mind focused on God and to have Him at the center of your household. There are no timid spirits allowed!

A woman's spirit affects her whole house. We have the power to instill peace, love, and joy in our homes. We also have the amazing opportunity to encourage our husbands and children to be closer to the Lord. What we say is extremely influential, and our moods can dramatically affect the flow of the home. Proverbs 21:9 (ISV) says, "It's better to live in a corner of a roof than to share a house with

a contentious woman." Wow! That is a very convicting verse for me. I do not want my husband or kids to ever feel that they would rather live in a corner on the roof than in my home. It would break my heart! However, all too often, I lose my temper or challenge my husband in front of our kids, which absolutely destroys the peacefulness of our home.

My prayer for you is to see the incredible honor it is to have a home. God has gifted you with one of His best blessings—a family to love and care for and to guide towards Him. During those especially exhausting moments, simply look at your kids. By truly looking at those beautiful children, who cherish every moment in their mama's presence, you will quickly be reminded of what's important. Focus less on *what* is on the table and more on *who* is around the table.

Every household is so vastly different. Do not look to others and make comparisons. Put your blinders on and you do you! You are the best wife for your husband, and you are the best mom for your children.

Questions to Ponder

- I want you to think about yourself as a homemaker. What are your natural strengths and weaknesses? Journal your thoughts for a few minutes.
- Now, how can you lean on the Holy Spirit in regards to your weaknesses? How can you use your strengths to create a more peaceful home?

Faith-Filled Ideas

Looking at your strengths and weaknesses from above, let's strategize together! For example, I am naturally organized and good at staying on top of the "clutter" in my home. However, I am horrible at deep-cleaning my house. When I finally get up the strength to complete a hard task, I listen to worship music very loudly to keep my mind focused and in a joyful state.

Another challenge I have for you is in regards to creating an environment of warmth and comfort in your home. During the next month, invite a friend and her children over for a playdate or host friends for dinner...and do it when your house is not in flawless condition! Leave some clutter on the counter, keep a few toys out, and run a little behind on serving the food. During all of this, pray for a spirit of thanksgiving for your home, your friends, and your family. Realize that the people coming to your house are coming to see you and not to be amazed by your cooking. Your home can be warm and inviting without being perfectly tidy.

Journal

_____

_____

_____

_____

_____

_____

_____

_____

She watches over the affairs of her household and does not eat the bread of idleness. Her children arise and call her blessed; her husband also, and he praises her: 'Many women do noble things, but you surpass them all.'
~ Proverbs 31: 27-29

"The habits of the child produce the character of the man."
~ Charlotte Mason

- It's time to meet with your Jesus. He is the One who loves you and knows your every need before you even speak one word. Come to Him in faith as His daughter. He is with you and is closer than your very breath. Ask Him to speak to you. He will!

- Read Proverbs 31:10-31. Write verses 27-29 in your journal.

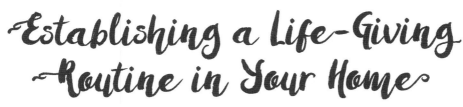

Establishing a Life-Giving Routine in Your Home

By: Deb Weakly

Once upon a time, I was a mom with littles. I remember how much fun it was to have young children in my home; it was a sweet and precious time in my life. As I was praying about this Bible study for our section on homemaking, I felt the Lord guiding me towards sharing about a life-giving routine that leads to a more peaceful and joy-filled home.

When I speak of a life-giving routine, I do not mean a rigid schedule. The type of routine I am talking about is more like a rhythm. A rhythm feels peaceful, not controlling. It allows for illnesses or a friend coming over to play. If the family has a chance to go to a movie together, the children can stay up a little later and enjoy some special family time. When we rule over our schedule instead of allowing our schedule to rule over us, we can enjoy spur-of-the-moment fun activities, knowing that the schedule will return to normal in a day or two. A rhythm helps you enjoy your life and the moments God brings across your path. It also helps your children feel safe and secure when they know what comes next and what to expect within their days.

Here are a few tips for your family on how to establish a life-giving routine in your home:

1. **Mornings in your home should be pleasant.** Greeting your children with a smile and telling them you are glad to see them creates a joy-filled start for their day. Put worship music on in their rooms as you wake them up and tell them, "This is the day the LORD has made. We will rejoice and be glad in it" (Psalm 118:24 NKJV). Help your children learn to love mornings from a young age. As with everything else, you set the tone in your home. Make sure the mornings feel joyful! This may be challenging if you have been up all night with a sick child or couldn't sleep for some reason. In my experience, spending a few minutes with God first thing in the morning, even when I was tired, helped me to be a better mom. Time reading the Word, praying, and committing my day to God, equipped me to enjoy my children and accomplish all God had for me that day.

2. **To help your mornings go more smoothly, set the breakfast table the night before.** Make sure you have what you need to enjoy a lovely meal together, even if it's simple. Be sure to pray with your children for their day and read a little devotion from a children's Bible. It's a great way to start the day!

3. **After breakfast, if you take your kids to school, do so while listening to a fun kids worship CD in the car.** We made it a point to only listen to children's worship music or books on tape in the car when we drove with the kids. When we dropped them off at any activity, we would tell them to "Go M.A.D!" meaning "**G**o **M**ake **A D**ifference!" Doing this helped our kids be mindful that they could make a difference for the Kingdom of God, no matter their age.

4. **If you homeschool, make sure your school hours are spent with as much prayerful peace as possible.** In our home, we read out loud a lot! But that didn't mean our kids were simply sitting like little cherubs at the kitchen table while mommy read. No, we gave them delicious tea and hot cocoa as well as many crafts to construct while I read to them: Lego's, knitting, sewing, puzzles, playdough, or watercolors. We made sure to allocate a budget each month for trips to Hobby Lobby for the kids. Both of our children are extremely creative to this day and have fond memories of our reading time.

5. **Have quiet time in the afternoon.** When our children grew out of their naps, we gave them the choice to sleep, read, or listen to a audiobook in their rooms for an hour while I rested in my room. Our daughter says that these were some of her best homeschooling times and that she loved that hour of resting and reading great books! Our son would quietly play with Legos in his room and listen to Adventures in Odyssey. He loved this time as well!

6. **Make family dinners a priority.** Establish a time for regular family dinners with no TV. Carve out time to eat together, even if you have sports or other activities, and make sure to ask questions of each other to get the conversation going. In our home, we always asked the question, "What's the best thing that happened to you today?" or "High/Low," which meant, "What was the best and the most challenging part of your day?" These questions helped us connect with one another and to linger at the table a little while longer. The dinner hour should be a sweet memory of your child's life. When dinner is over, everyone helps pick up and clean. Put on some fun, active music and dance around the kitchen together as you clean.

7. **If you have babies, begin to gently establish a consistent bedtime routine.** I know there are a lot of schools of thought out there, but some of my husband's and my sweetest memories are rocking and singing our babies to sleep. Looking back, if we did contribute to negative sleep habits for our babies by rocking them to sleep, the fact that we felt very close to them and they to us overruled the little bit of lost sleep. But, as with everything else in Help Club, "You do you!" If it works better for your babies to lay them down instead of rocking, go for it! Do what's best for your family. You can sing to your baby as you change diapers and while you feed them too!

   Also, be sure to have realistic expectations for your baby's sleep habits. Don't be angry or grouchy with your baby because he or she is not sleeping like your friend's baby. Let. It. Go! I assure you that your children will outgrow getting up at night. Be like Dory from *Finding Nemo* and "Just keep swimming!" Continue to be consistent, knowing all things take time, and soon your baby will outgrow the need to wake up at night.

8. **Create a fun bedtime routine for your children!** Be sure to begin bathtime and bedtime early enough to where you can take your time putting your children to bed. The bedtime hour should be one associated with a sweetness of spending time with mom and dad. In our home, we read countless books to our kids at night. Randy even read science encyclopedias filled with pictures to our daughter, Christie. As a child, science was her passion, and she is now happily employed as a software engineer. They also read through all of the C.S. Lewis children's books.

9. **Let your kids listen to fun books on tape after you tuck them in.** You will need to account for this in your bedtime routine. We put our kids to bed 20 minutes earlier so they could listen to their favorite CD's such as:

   - *Wee Sing Bible Songs* (both of our children gave their lives to Jesus while listening to this). They are now available on iTunes.
   - *Classical Kids Collection* (Kid friendly stories about famous classical composers).
   - *Adventures in Odyssey* (From Focus in the Family).
   - *Your Story Hour* (Uncle Dan and Aunt Carole tell a variety of stories, from Bible stories to American History stories).

10. **Don't sign your kids up for too many activities!** One per child is plenty! Resist the urge to schedule every moment of your child's life. Trust me, it's not worth it. A child needs time to simply be a child.

Questions to Ponder

- How is the atmosphere of your home? Do your kids have a lot of meltdowns? What can you change in your home to make it less stressful? Are you too busy, especially at night? Do your children need more downtime at home?

Faith-Filled Ideas

What is one idea from today's study that you can begin to implement in your home this week? Adding or changing one habit is usually doable, but don't try to do too much all at one time. Maybe add one new change or habit every week or two. Give your family time to adjust.

journal

_____

_____

_____

_____

_____

_____

_____

_____

_____

_____

But one thing is necessary, Mary has chosen the good portion, which will not be taken away from her.

~ Luke 10:42 (ESV)

"We need to find God, and he cannot be found in noise and restlessness. God is the friend of silence. See how nature—trees, flowers, grass—grows in silence; see the stars, the moon and the sun, how they move in silence...We need silence to be able to touch souls."
~ Mother Teresa

- Be still and quiet before the Lord. Ask the Lord for ears to hear His voice.

- Read Luke 10:38-42. Write verses 40 & 42 in your journal.

- Ask the Lord for insight into what "the better portion" is.

A Wise Woman Listens

By: Jennifer Kindle

A wise woman builds her home not only with her hands but with her ears tuned into the Father's still, small voice. One evening, the Lord spoke into my heart specifically concerning one of my young adult children. What He said about my son was so very specific that I wasn't sure if it was my idea or if He had actually told me this. I knew if it was an idea I formed on my own, I would allow myself to become accusatory, putting a wedge between my son and me rather than drawing our hearts closer to one another. I asked the Lord to prepare my heart to respond rather than react.

Two days went by, and my son came to me, asked if we could talk, and told me he had something to tell me. Immediately, I prayed that my facial expressions and response to whatever he was about to disclose would be full of gentleness and grace. We stood there, a split second passed, and he admitted that he wasn't sure he could talk to me about this situation. He asked if I would just ask the Lord to reveal it to me so he wouldn't have to say it.

My children have this habit of trusting that I hear from the Lord, so it's very normal when they ask this of me. I agreed, and before I could even pray, the Lord nudged my heart and reminded me that He already told me two days prior.

I admitted to my child that I knew what he wanted to talk to me about because the Lord had told me two days prior and brought it to my mind again as we stood there together. I shared specifically what the Lord had spoken to me concerning him, and it was exactly what my child could not bring himself to tell me. Through this situation, our hearts were drawn closer to one another and deeper into trust for Jesus.

That same evening before we climbed into bed, this child, way beyond the age of snuggling with his mom, came and hugged me, telling me he was very thankful that he could talk to me about anything.

That night solidified my belief in the Lord's ability to work in our children's lives through our obedience to listen.

As women who have a heart to wisely build our homes for the glory of God, we must first become women who create space for the Holy Spirit to breathe into our days. We cannot hear the heart of the Father until we habitually take time to sit in His presence without distractions. I believe we can be busy with our daily duties and still be quiet and still in our souls, keeping ourselves aware of His presence.

Moms with young children may not be able to realistically create a space that is quiet and free from distractions, but we can tune our ears to listen for the nudge of the Spirit. Our eyes can be fixed with anticipation to see through the filter of God's desires. We can become wise women who build our homes by diligently building up our faith as we practice hearing the voice of God in our days.

I want to bravely proclaim that we have the ability to know the heart of the Father concerning our children. The Lord so graciously spoke into my soul over my own child because He promises to gently lead those with young (Isaiah 40:11), and He wants my response to my child to be loving, gentle, and kind. He led me to reflect His heart towards my own child by graciously speaking into my life, and I believe the reason He allowed me to hear His voice is because He has taught me to ask Him.

We are desperate—desperate people, desperate women, desperate moms. We cannot build wisely without the help of the Holy Spirit. The Spirit is a gift to us from the Father; He is our helper, our counselor, and our guide. I encourage you to ask Him for help today; ask Him for ears to hear and eyes to see.

Questions to Ponder

• How often am I clear in hearing God's heart concerning me and my children?

• Am I spending more time listening to the voices of culture or practicing hearing the voice of God?

• Where can I carve out time and create space for the Holy Spirit to breathe into my day?

Faith-Filled Ideas

Carve out space on your calendar to practice being still and quiet, waiting on the Lord to speak to you. Begin by inviting Him into that moment by asking Him to speak. Ask Him to help you stay focused and give you the words to ask Him. It pleases Him to answer the prayers you've prayed, the ones that He has asked you to pray, so patiently wait for Him to give you the words to ask.

Invite your children into a time of quiet before the Lord and help them practice waiting, expecting God to speak.

Take a walk with your children, inviting the Holy Spirit to come along. Ask for ears to hear what He wants to speak into your hearts as you stroll along through His creation.

Take a few moments throughout the day, pause with your children, and invite the Spirit to help you to be aware of His presence. Wait until He speaks into the moment, and share what you heard with one another.

Journal

Food for the Soul

As a stay-at-home mom of five, my family adheres to a tight grocery budget. I am constantly looking for ways to make delicious, filling, healthy meals that don't break the bank. Beans and rice are a staple in our family, but sometimes it's nice to find a recipe that will bring dinnertime up a notch.

Homemade Chicken Gnocchi Soup is just that recipe! It's so impressive, you would never imagine how inexpensive it is to make. I will warn you, though, this isn't a 30-minute meal. It is a bit laborious, making stock from scratch and homemade gnocchi, but the result is well worth the time invested.

When thinking about this recipe, I am reminded of the Proverbs 31 woman. We are told that she "works with eager hands," "provides food for her family," and has arms that "are strong for her tasks." As women of Christ, we strive daily to fill these roles. By being good stewards of our families' budgets and blessing our families with a meal infused with love, we are serving Christ as modern day Proverbs 31 women. Proverbs 31:27, 30-31a says "She watches over the affairs of her household and does not eat the bread of idleness. Charm is deceptive, beauty is fleeting, but a woman who fears the Lord is to be praised. Honor her for all that her hands have done."

HOMEMADE CHICKEN GNOCCHI SOUP

By: Brandi Carson

CHICKEN BROTH

Ingredients:

3-4 pounds chicken drumsticks, breasts, thighs, or wings

1 large or 2 small onions, coarsely chopped

3-4 carrots, coarsely chopped

3-4 stalks of celery, coarsely chopped

Salt and pepper to taste

Directions:

1. Coarsely chop onions, carrots, and celery. Place the veggies and chicken in a large stockpot and cover with a couple inches of water.

2. Boil for 20-30 minutes until chicken is thoroughly cooked.

3. Remove chicken and let cool until able to handle. Turn heat down to medium.

4. Remove chicken from the bone and shred.

5. Return the bones to the broth and vegetable mixture, and bring to a boil.

6. Simmer on medium-low heat with the lid on for several hours. Add water if needed.

7. Strain the broth and let cool. Now you have a nice yummy broth ready for soup.

GNOCCHI

Ingredients:

3-4 large russet potatoes, peeled but left whole

1 egg

2-3 cups all-purpose flour

¼- ⅓ cup freshly grated parmesan cheese (optional)

3-4 cups homemade chicken stock

Directions:

1. In a medium pot, boil whole potatoes for 30-45 minutes or until you can stick a fork in them.

2. Drain potatoes.

3. Place potatoes back in the pot, and cook on medium heat for a couple minutes to evaporate any excess water.

4. Remove potatoes and let cool.

5. While potatoes cool, finely grate the cheese in a medium bowl.

6. With a fine grater, grate the potatoes. They will be light and fluffy.

7. Add salt, pepper, and the egg. Mix lightly with a fork.

8. Slowly add flour a little at a time while mixing with a fork until a dough consistency forms. If sticky, add more flour.

9. Dust countertop with flour and turn dough out onto it. Knead a of couple times to make sure the dough is well mixed. Slightly knead into a ball.

10. Working in small sections, roll the dough into a rope about a half-inch thick.

11. Cut into half-inch pieces and dust lightly with flour to keep from sticking, repeat.

12. In a medium saucepan bring the chicken stock to a boil.

13. Gently drop gnocchi into boiling stock a handful at a time, and boil for a few minutes until they float. You know they are done when they pop up and float!

14. When they are floating, using a slotted spoon, remove gnocchi from chicken stock and place onto a sheet pan, repeat.

15. This recipe will make more gnocchi than you need, so freeze the extra on the sheet pan. When they are frozen solid, transfer them to a freezer bag for your next soup day!

You just made homemade gnocchi, way to go!

CHICKEN GNOCCHI SOUP

Ingredients:

1 recipe of homemade chicken stock

1-2 cups of shredded chicken

3-4 cloves of garlic, minced

2 small or 1 large onion, diced

1 ½ cups shredded carrots

1 ½ cups celery, diced

½ cup frozen spinach, diced

1-pint half and half

2-3 tsp. dried rosemary

Salt and pepper to taste

A couple tablespoons of flour

Directions:

1. On medium heat, saute onions and garlic in olive oil until soft. Add celery and carrots and continue cooking until softened.

2. Add a couple more tablespoons of oil, or even butter, and heat through. Add 2-3 tablespoons of flour to make a roux. Cook for a minute or two, stirring frequently.

3. Add stock, stirring the bottom well to mix thoroughly and to get all the bits off the bottom. Add salt, pepper, and rosemary.

4. Stir constantly so nothing sticks to the bottom, and bring to a boil until thickened.

5. Once the soup starts thickening, add chicken, spinach, and gnocchi.

6. Turn down the heat and add half and half. Don't let it boil.

7. Continue to simmer without boiling for another 15-20 minutes or so. Always check the salt and pepper before serving!

Mom Tips:

• A great time to make stock and gnocchi is when you can get chicken and potatoes on sale. I usually wait until the chicken is on sale for 99 cents/lb. and the potatoes are 99 cents for a 10 lb. bag!

• An easy alternative is to place the bones, water, and vegetables in your crockpot and cook on high for 8 hours or low for 12+ hours.

• Disclaimer: You can totally use store-bought broth for this recipe, but making it from scratch is a cost effective way to get the most bang for your buck.

• There is more chicken than you need for this recipe so save half and freeze it in a zipper bag for the next time you want to make this soup or another meal!

• With this recipe you have made extra chicken and gnocchi so you have most of the ingredients in the freezer ready to go. The next time you want to make it just buy boxed broth and veggies and you are ready to go! Simmer for another 15-20 minutes, season to taste with salt and pepper.

Journal

Homemaking

~ Week Two ~

"But the plans of the Lord stand firm forever, the purposes of his heart through all generations."
~ Psalm 33:11

Hello My Friend,

How is your heart this week? How is your walk with Jesus? I find that as I learn to draw closer to the Lord, my heart towards my home changes. I see my children and husband in the light of His grace. My outlook on my responsibilities within our family becomes one of joy and intentionality instead of duty, exhaustion, and guilt.

Do you find yourself feeling empty as a wife and mother, and lacking the desire to seek the Lord? I do too at times. During these times, let's pray that God would give us a renewed desire for Him, for His Word, and for relationship with our loving Savior. He wants to give you purpose and joy within the four walls of your home, as you walk out your calling each day!

I don't know about you, but at times I can be my own worst enemy within my home. Sometimes I feel as if my family deserves more than my meager offerings. I'm not overly gifted in curating a perfect home, and it can be challenging to keep up with the messiness of raising kids. But as I run after the Lord, or maybe more accurately stumble in His direction, He changes me. As I humble my heart before my beloved Father, He is opening my eyes to His grace. And, with that, the whole of my home is bathed in the glorious light of this grace and what I have to offer somehow becomes enough.

Mama, your dear ones need you. In fact, *you* are exactly what they need. As you seek Him, God is taking you, just as you are and bathing you, your home, everything and everyone around you, with His beautiful grace. And *that*, my friends, is truly the light and joy of the home!

Seek Him today, and do not give up! A life of joy within your home and a baptism of the Lord's perfect grace in the mundane awaits you! Keep going, sister!

Love in Him,
Tara Davis and the Help Club for Moms Team

❝ *God answers the mess of life with one word: 'Grace.'* **❞**
~ *Max Lucado*

Mom Tips

By: Leslie Leonard

"Let your speech always be with grace, seasoned with salt, that you may know how you ought to answer each other." ~ Colossians 4:6 (NKJV)

The Wise Woman Builds Her Spirit

• Write Proverbs 24:3-4 on your notecards or in dry erase marker on your bathroom mirror or record it on your phone. Try to memorize these verses by the end of the week.

• Listen to a Help Club for Moms video from our Facebook page and journal about what you learned.

The Wise Woman Loves Her Husband

• Give your husband a break from his "Honey Do List" this week. Suggest that he meet with a friend for dinner or coffee to recharge his batteries.

• At the end of each day this week, take a moment to reconnect with your husband. Talk about your day, watch a movie, or play a game. Meaningful conversations between husband and wife will help strengthen your bond of intimacy.

The Wise Woman Loves Her Children

• Write Colossians 3:23 on your chalkboard or a notecard and place it in an area of the house that you frequent. Have your children repeat the verse every time they come into the room. Make a goal for everyone to have it memorized by the end of the week.

• Do the "15 minute pick up" with your children right before your husband comes home for the day. Set a timer for 15 minutes; pick up everything that is out of place and put it away. Focus on the shared living areas of your home and have everyone help. You get a clutter-free home, and your husband gets to come home to a picked-up house with everyone in a great mood.

The Wise Woman Cares For Her Home

• Make your bed every morning this week, as soon as you wake up. While you are making your bed, pray about your upcoming day and commit it to the Lord. Ask Him to bless your day and turn over any concerns you have to Him.

• Set the table for dinner every night this week. Commit to eating together as a family by creating a specific space to come together. Enlist help from your children too!

> " She is clothed with strength and dignity; she can laugh at the days to come.
> She speaks with wisdom, and faithful instruction is on her tongue. She watches
> over the affairs of her household and does not eat the bread of idleness.
> Her children arise and call her blessed; her husband also, and he praises her:
> 'Many women do noble things, but you surpass them all.' "
>
> ~ Proverbs 31:25-30

"I believe that a godly home is a foretaste of heaven. Our homes, imperfect as they are, must be a haven from the chaos outside. They should be a reflection of our eternal home, where troubled souls find peace, weary hearts find rest, hungry bodies find refreshment, lonely pilgrims find communion, and wounded spirits find compassion."
~ Jani Ortlund

- Call your prayer partner for your 10-minute prayer call! Keep trying to connect until you get to pray together. This tiny habit of praying regularly with a friend will truly change your life!

- Cherished daughter, come rest at the feet of the King of Kings today! Pray and ask God to speak to you through His Word as you spend time in His presence. Read Proverbs 31:10-31.

Home: A Pleasant Place

By: Rebekah Measmer

What is homemaking? Google defines it as "the creation and management of a home, especially as a pleasant place in which to live."

Confession time here. Honestly, my home is not always a pleasant place to live. The reason for this has very little to do with whether or not the rooms within are trendy and organized. It has nothing to do with whether the mountain of clean (or dirty) laundry has been taken care of, what is or isn't in my refrigerator, or what is or isn't in my children's toy bin. Rather, it has everything to do with me, and—spoiler alert—it has everything to do with you, too!

As wives and mothers, whether we stay at home or work outside the home, we are responsible for the atmosphere in our homes. The Bible says, "The wise woman builds her house, but with her own hands the foolish one tears hers down" (Proverbs 14:1). We are the builders of our home, but we can also wreak havoc with thoughtless words or actions.

Countless times, in hurt and anger, I have flung foolish words at my husband or children, regretting them the moment they escaped my lips. Too frequently, I have grunted greetings rather than verbalized them, and, absorbed in my own little world, I have missed opportunities to show love to my family. If, like me, you have fallen short of the Proverbs 31 woman, take heart because there is no condemnation for those who are in Christ (Romans 8:1). However, "no condemnation" does not give us a free license for poor habits.

One habit that I had to change was staying up late at night. I had to start going to bed when my husband went to bed shortly after our children were tucked in for the night. I learned early on as a parent that if I didn't get to bed before 10 p.m., I was a wreck the following day, and my children had to deal with a grouchy, easily annoyed, or easily discouraged mama. While the Bible doesn't say anything specific about when a proper bedtime should be, it has much to say about choosing wisdom and how miserable a home is with a cantankerous wife (Proverbs 21:9). The Bible even goes so far as to say that it is better to have nothing but a dry crust to eat in peace and quiet than a house full of feasting and strife (Proverbs 17:1).

A daily quiet time before my kids woke for the day was another routine I began. While I love my sleep, I know I need my Savior even more! For "unless the LORD builds the house, the builders labor in vain. Unless the LORD watches over the city, the guards stand watch in vain" (Psalm 127:1). No matter how hard I try to be the perfect wife and mother, creating a beautiful home and whipping up delicious dishes in my kitchen, I will always fall short of the mark without Christ.

It is through the power of Jesus Christ and the Holy Spirit in our lives that we can speak with love, wisdom, and kindness, practicing patience and grace instead of severity. When you make a mistake, apologize immediately and move on. Your husband and children will cherish a loving and attentive women much more than the best toys or home that money can buy, and your home will truly become a pleasant place to live.

Questions to Ponder

• Are there habits in my life or routines that I need to change in order to bless my family?

• Am I getting enough rest each night so I can be rested and awake before my children each day?

• What type of atmosphere do I want my husband and children to come home to?

Faith-Filled Ideas

As a couple or a family, make a list of family values and frame a printed copy in a high-traffic area of your home. We have a list of family rules in our living room and a list of kitchen rules in our dining area with rules such as "No Cell Phones Allowed [during mealtime]" and "Be Thankful."

In your own words, write Proverbs 31:10-31 in your journal. Whether you believe it or not, you ARE a Proverbs 31 woman, so own it! Pray through the passage, replacing "she" with "me."

Example: *"Lord, thank you for making me a wife of noble character. Thank you for seeing the value in me. Thank you that my family has complete confidence in me and my abilities, and they lack for nothing. Thank you for helping me bring good and not harm to those around me, and thank you for giving me the strength and energy to do your work today..."*

Journal

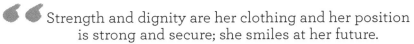

Strength and dignity are her clothing and her position
is strong and secure; she smiles at her future.
~ Proverbs 31:25 (AMP)

"Lord, let our house be something more than just a shelter with a door; May its windows glow with light, shedding radiance through the night. Not just a glitter of glass and chrome, but give it the feel of a happy home."
~ Christine White

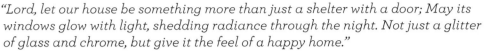

- Come join me as we explore homemaking. What does it mean? What should we prioritize? I would love to share a story with you about my journey through these questions. Pull up a chair, even if it is covered with blankets or toys or toast crumbs!

- Read Proverbs 31. Write verse 25 in your journal.

When Life Gets Messy

By: Julie Maegdlin

I have a confession to make. I do not like to clean. I really, really do not like to clean. I will do just about anything to avoid cleaning the toilets and showers. And dusting just makes me sneeze, so I avoid that at all costs. Vacuuming means I have to get stuff off the floor, and that is a huge task. Besides, I have heard that having dog hair all over the place may actually strengthen your immune system. I'm not sure about the validity of that claim, but who am I to argue?

I haven't always felt this way. When my husband and I were first married, I enjoyed cleaning our little townhome. There were only two of us living there, and we both worked full time. My husband is as neat as can be. It wasn't very challenging to keep our first home tidy and sparkling.

Today, however, is a different story. We have a bigger house in which we have raised two daughters and two dogs. In the past 21 years that we have lived here, we have had countless parties, dinners, and gatherings with friends and family. In this home, we have laughed and cried and everything in between. A beautiful life we have lived here, but it has been a messy one. And the house has reflected those messes.

Cleaning became more and more of a challenge for me after having a family. It was so much easier to stash something in a corner of the room than to put it away. Piling clean laundry on the spare bed became the norm during holidays, at the beginning of the school year, the end of the school year, summers...You get my point. It was simply too much effort during some weeks to fold, iron, hang, and put away. I figured that at least I ran the washer and dryer! I gave myself grace. I wanted to be there for my family in so many ways that I didn't take the time to maintain the basics of our home.

Storms in life happen to all of us. And storms are meant to be survived. I don't shovel my driveway during a blizzard; I make sure my family is warm and fed and that the pipes don't freeze. Those are priorities. When life gets messy, little ones get sick, or we all are in need of sleep, I don't worry about cleaning my baseboards. I make sure we are nourished and rested and cared for—again, priorities.

I was in a life-storm for about six years. It didn't let up. In trying to survive, we let the messes happen. We let the piles grow. We let our dog sit on the sofa because cuddling with a puppy was more important than a hair-free sofa. We had fun when we could instead of staying home and cleaning out the corners. Now, I am just coming out of the storm and looking around at the damage. Whoa. The aftermath is not pretty. It's overwhelming. I don't like to clean in the first place, and now I am facing this.

Storms do pass. Eventually, the sun comes out and it's time to get back to work. The driveway must be shoveled. The floor must be mopped to remove the footprints tracked in by the snow. Family and friends must be fed and restored.

One day at a time, I will get through this mess. I want to restore my home to a place of beauty. When I do, I know it will be even lovelier than before the storm hit. This home is filled with more love and more laughter than ever. I took care of the priorities. Now is the time of restoration.

There is a season for everything. Take care of your home when you can. Take care of your family's needs first. Bless them with a clean bathroom and a well-stocked pantry. It all matters. Just take it one day at a time.

Questions to Ponder

- What are your priorities? Are you aware of what needs to be done and how much time you have to dedicate to that task?
- Are you keeping up with the daily tasks of taking care of your home? Are you giving yourself grace when you are doing your best but it doesn't seem to be enough? God is enough. Lean on Him.

Faith-Filled Ideas

Plan your week. Plan your meals, your errands, your cleaning needs, and your time for fun. Enlist the help of your children. Everyone can have a part in keeping the home as orderly as possible.

journal

_____
_____
_____
_____
_____
_____
_____
_____

'Martha, Martha,' the Lord answered, 'you are worried and upset about many things, but few things are needed—or indeed only one. Mary has chosen what is better, and it will not be taken away from her.'
~ Luke 10:41-42

"I can use the house to create a home. I can offer my family, my friends, myself, and even strangers the gift of love by making them feel special when they are in my home."
~ Sarah Mae

- Read Luke 10:38-42.

- Journal about your home. If a stranger were to come into your home, what three words would she use to describe it?

Making a Home

By: Krystle Porter

As I sit here writing this study and gleaning inspiration from the Lord, He tells me to write from my heart in this season I'm in. Allow me to give you a little glimpse of my life currently.

I am a mother of four, soon to be five, children. I'm 16 weeks pregnant! In this season, I have been struggling with all-day pregnancy sickness—worse than ever! I have also been homeschooling two of my children and working a part-time job from home. Given my situation, the idea of writing a study on homemaking made me chuckle, to be honest! My home has not been tidy, my toilets have rings, and my floors could use about an entire day of deep cleaning...did I mention the laundry is in one giant heap that resembles Mount Everest?!

As I thought about homemaking, I was struck with this thought: What if homemaking isn't about having a tidy, Martha Stewart home? What if homemaking is more about the heart? Breaking it down, I would prefer to call it "making a home." Ahhhhh...doesn't that sound much more manageable? I sure think so. When I think of making my home, I think of the ways I want my home to feel: kind, warm, graceful, loving, forgiving, affectionate, and all the things that make a home comfortable and safe. I want my home to be a place where my family can rest, a place where they can retreat, a place where they can fill their love tanks!

I don't know about you, but often, my go-to homemaking attempts are just me barking at my children to clean their rooms, huffing and puffing as I try to get "all the things" done. In those moments, homemaking isn't fun; it's stressful!

Proverbs 24:3-4 (ESV) says, "By wisdom a house is built, and by understanding it is established; by knowledge the rooms are filled with all the precious and pleasant riches."

Last night, I sat in my girls' room and read them one of their favorite chapter books, *Nancy Clancy*. Their room was a MESS! But in the moment, I chose to overlook the mess, literally push toys and clothes to the side to make a space for me to sit, and just read to them without saying a word!

My oldest said, "Oh Mommy! You haven't read to us in a while! I'm so happy you are reading to us tonight!"

I could have missed my opportunity to bless my girls by forcing them to clean, but I focused on "making my home" instead of homemaking. This moment was a perfect example of the verse above! I want to build my home with wisdom, understanding, and knowledge, which yield pleasant riches!

As we reflect on the verses featuring Mary and Martha from our reading above, we should think about what Jesus said: "...few things are needed—or indeed only one. Mary has chosen what is better and it will not be taken away from her." Mama, choose what is better. Jesus cares so much about our hearts and our children's hearts. Don't miss opportunities to "make your home" while you are preoccupied with homemaking chores. The dishes, laundry, and messes will return tomorrow anyway—you can count on that!

Questions to Ponder

• As we began today's study, we journaled about what three words we thought a stranger may use to describe our home, but now, think about what you would like those three words to be! How do you want your home to feel to your family, friends, and guests?

• What are a few things in your home that are taking a higher priority than they should? These are the things that keep you distracted and grumpy in your home, preventing you from being able to "make a home".

• What are some ways you can make your home feel lighter, happier, or more inviting not only for you, but for your family too?

Faith-Filled Ideas

One thing that has helped me to have a bigger perspective in my home is writing Bible verses on a chalkboard for the whole family to see! My chalkboard is large and noticeable, and I find God often uses it to change my focus when my day takes a turn for the worst. Chalkboards are super easy to make (check Pinterest!), and you can choose the size you want. Or, you can just purchase a ready-made one to avoid the hassle of making one! A white board would work as well.

Write and frame a family mission statement. For example, "In this home there is love, acceptance, grace, forgiveness, kindness, respect..." And the list goes on! This will establish the atmosphere of your home and serve as a reminder for you and your guests. I love seeing these in homes, and it is such a fun family project to work on together!

journal

_____

_____

_____

_____

journal

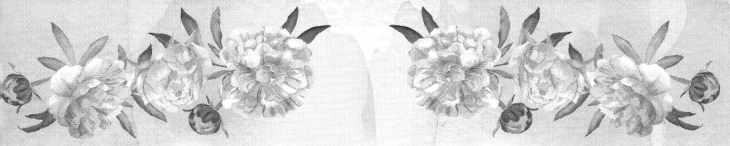

Everyday Celebrations:

Making Each Day Special

By: Tara Davis

Hey mama! Do you ever feel weighed down by the mundane duties of life? Me too! But I want to constantly lay my weary heart before Jesus and let Him fill me with joy and purpose in a new way. I want to be a mom who enjoys each day with the little people God has placed in my life! I want to fill our home to the brim with laughter, grace, and God's Word! I want to put a drop of special in each ordinary day! And the benefit of all this? My kiddos listen better, even during times they generally don't want to. When I am a mom who reaches their hearts with fun, I see them respond more readily to messages I so desperately want to teach them—the messages of Jesus, His love, and His plans for their lives.

Do you want to fill your home with an extra dose of joy too? A fun-loving mama tills fertile soil in the hearts of her children into which she is able to plant seeds of God's love, grace, forgiveness, and holiness. Join us in having fun with our kids today! There are so many ways to engage your children's hearts, and everyday celebrations is just one of them. Here are a few simple everyday celebration ideas to enjoy with your kids today!

- **Stargazing Party** – Grab some blankets and pillows and set them up outside for a night your kids will love! Make some hot cocoa and enjoy laying outside together watching the night sky! See if you can find constellations and shooting stars. Talk about the vast beauty of God's creation.

- **Dance Party** – Turn on some music and have fun with your kids. To really pump up the fun, grab some dollar store glow necklaces and have a dance party in the dark!

- **Unbirthday Party** – Make a simple treat, even a scoop of ice cream with a candle will do. Wrap up something from around your house (an old toy that was a favorite, a bottle of bubbles, even something silly like a hairbrush or the television remote control), and listen to *A Very Merry Unbirthday Song* (you can find it right here: https://bit.ly/2JQ2Jdi). Then, grab the treat you just made, and sneak around the house to the front door. Ring the doorbell, turn on the music, and surprise your little ones with a silly unbirthday celebration!

Everyday Celebrations:
Making Each Day Special

- **National Fort Building Day Party** – National Fort Building Day is not actually a real holiday, but you sure can pretend it is one! Let your kids build the fort of their dreams with your help! Use couch cushions, blankets, sheets, furniture, boxes—the sky is the limit! Hang some Christmas lights inside, bring some snacks or books, and spend time in the fort with them.

- **Snuggle Party** – Grab some blankets (my kids like to make a giant nest with them for all of us) and snuggle. Talk, read books, or play a game to make the snuggle party special, but the main purpose is just to lavish a bit of love on your kids!

- **Special Movie Night Party** – Pull the mattresses off your kids' beds (or use an air mattress) and put them all together in front of your television for a special movie night! Pop some popcorn or do a little snack buffet in the kitchen with food you have on hand and make the night extra fun!

- **Pizza Party** – This is no ordinary pizza party, though you could turn it into one if you would like! Gather your kids and check out the book *Pete's a Pizza* by William Steig (you can watch the book being read right here: **https://bit.ly/2qluRy2**). Then make your kids into pizzas! All you will need is some torn up paper for cheese and maybe a sprinkle of flour. Your kids will think it is hilarious!

Pray and ask the Lord how to connect with your children's hearts in an extra special way. Be sure to tell them each day about God's love and about how much you love them too!

Love Your Husband

~ Week One ~

"A loving doe, a graceful deer..."
~ Proverbs 5:19a

Dearest Mama,

I love reading anything by Ruth Bell Graham, the Reverend Billy Graham's wife. Over the years, her writings have inspired me, convicted me, and caused me to want to love my husband and children well. I appreciate learning from older and wiser women like Ruth, who have a way of driving a point home sweetly, but with the touch of a velvet hammer. Her words cause you to stop dead in your tracks, but always give you hope in the exhortation.

I remember reading today's quote from Ruth as a young wife, feeling the admonishment to stop the process of nagging my husband about his faults and instead making the decision in my heart to simply make him happy. How many times do we wives fix our gaze on all of the habits and quirks of our men, instead of praying earnestly for them to feel the love of Jesus and asking the Lord to help us to be a respectful, encouraging wife who loves to makes her husband happy?

How much more joyful would our little homes be if they were filled with the unconditional love of Jesus, and if our aim was to build up our men instead of tearing them down? There is still a need to be honest with our husbands when a situation arises, but when we are able to give up our expectations and control to the Lord, we can minister to our husbands and be a source of encouragement instead of criticism. We can then truly be like the "loving doe" and "graceful deer" whose husband is intoxicated with her love (Proverbs 5:19).

As we read through the studies for the next two weeks and learn how to love and respect our husbands well, may we ask the Lord to open our hearts, give us wisdom, and help us to make our husbands' lives a bit more happy, even if it's just in some little way. After all, Rome wasn't built in a day, and a good marriage can become great as we choose to love well one day at a time.

Blessings and love,
Deb Weakly and the Help Club for Moms Team

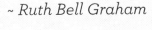

It's my job to love and respect Billy; it's God's job to make him good.
God called you not to make your husband good, but to make him happy.

~ *Ruth Bell Graham*

Mom Tips

By: Leslie Leonard

"Let all that you do be done in love."
~ 1 Corinthians 16:14 (NKJV)

The Wise Woman Builds Her Spirit

- Practice J.O.Y. this week. J.O.Y. is Jesus-Others-Yourself. Everywhere you go this week, the grocery store, your child's school, the coffee shop...apply this concept. Think of Jesus first, then others, and then yourself.

- Write Luke 1:45 on your notecards or in your journal. Take the time to memorize it by the end of the week.

The Wise Woman Loves Her Husband

- Acknowledge your husband and family as soon as they walk into the house by saying "hello" to them. These little things let them know that they matter to you. Let them know that your home is the *best* place to be because they are well-loved by their family. Teach your children to say hello to one another too!

- If your husband is grouchy or just a little bit off this week, instead of being offended and hurt, take the opportunity to pray a blessing over him. Pray that God would flood your husband's heart with His love, peace, and value. You are your husband's biggest prayer warrior. James 4:11 reminds us to not speak against one another.

The Wise Woman Loves Her Children

- Instead of catching your children being bad, catch your children being good this week. Every time you see one of your children acting or behaving in a good and positive way, stop and praise them. Remember to say thank you.

- Make a fun art project with your children this week. Pull out the paints and construction paper and see what fun creations you can come up with. Hang them up art-gallery-style and invite friends and family over to view the masterpieces.

The Wise Woman Cares For Her Home

- Sit down and plan meals for the week. Once you finish, write your grocery list.

- Clean and organize your laundry room. Wipe down and dust the cabinets and mop the floors. Take the time to run the clean/sanitize cycle on your washing machine.

Teach me your way, Lord, that I may rely on your faithfulness; give me an undivided heart, that I may fear your name.

~ Psalm 86:11

"God created marriage. No government subcommittee envisioned it. No social organization developed it. Marriage was conceived and born in the mind of God."
~ Max Lucado

- Call your prayer partner for your 10-minute prayer call! God is the one who has the power to work in your heart and the hearts of those you love. Prayer changes everything!

- Psalm 46:10 says, "Be still and know that I am God." Challenge yourself to quiet your heart today, and listen for the still, small voice of God as you begin your study time. Jeremiah 29:13 promises that we will find God when we seek Him with all of our heart.

- Read Ephesians 3:17-19. Stop, close your eyes, and let God capture your affection. Meditate on the breadth, length, height, and depth of His love for you. Paul says God's love is more than we can know. You are so very loved by God!

A Heart Undivided

By: Kristi Valentine

How is your heart, my friend? Let's be honest and look inward, deeply.

In Psalm 86:11, King David prays for an undivided heart. In Psalm 51:10, King David asks for a pure heart and a renewed, loyal spirit within him. King David wasn't perfect, but his heart pleased God (1 Samuel 13:14, Acts 13:22). I am desperate to please God! Are you? Are you praying for a pure, loyal, and undivided heart like David did? Are you open to God teaching you His way, even in your marriage?

We are able to follow God's design for our lives and marriages only if our hearts are pure, loyal, and undivided. His design for marriage is represented by the model of Christ and how He loved the church: Just like Christ is our leader, the husband is the "head of the wife" (Ephesians 5:23), and she is to submit to Him fully. Many times, this Biblical image seems so cliché and traditional to us that we dismiss its significance and, consequently, we don't consider the gravity of God's intentions for marriage.

Perhaps marriage and submission are very difficult subjects to broach because you have been wounded so severely in your marriage. Perhaps you are angry at your husband and angry at God. While writing this, I am stopping to pray for your heart. Your loving Father will carry you through the battlefield. Know that He is faithful (1 Corinthians 1:9) and can do more than you are able to think or imagine (Ephesians 3:20). Press into Him, receive His love and healing, and commit to following His path for you.

God is calling you to set your mind and your heart on Him, not on earthly things (Colossians 3:1-2). If you're like me, your thoughts are on your children, feelings, finances, body image, friendships, plans, food, exercise, movies, work, and the list goes on. Our minds and hearts are often so full that there is no room for God. Yet, in Matthew 6:25, Jesus tells us not to be anxious about our lives. We are in bondage, my friends! Slaves to the things of this world. But marriage is not of this world; it is ordained and designed by God. How can we achieve God's design for marriage, or any other part of our lives, if we aren't intentionally setting our hearts on Him?

Psalm 127:1a (NCV) warns, "If the Lord doesn't build the house, the builders are working for nothing." If we want a great marriage, but we choose to set our minds and hearts on the things of this earth, our hearts are divided, and we are striving for nothing.

Our cry to God needs to be like David's in the Psalms: "Create in me a clean heart, O God. Renew a loyal spirit within me. Restore to me the joy of your salvation, and make me willing to obey you" (Psalm 51:10, 12 NLT), even if it means obeying Your commandments about marriage. In my marriage, Lord, "give me happiness...for I give myself to you" (Psalm 86:4 NLT).

Questions to Ponder

- Read Matthew 6:25-33 (NLT). Jesus says, "Seek the Kingdom of God above all else, and live righteously, and He will give you *everything you need*." Ask God for a spirit of revelation as you ponder the enormity of that statement. What is He saying to you?

- Ephesians 3:20-21 (ESV) says, "Now to him who is able to do far more abundantly than all that we ask or think, according to the power at work within us, to him be glory in the church and in Christ Jesus throughout all generations, forever and ever." Be encouraged! Marriage is God's design, and so are you and your husband. Go to God and ask Him for a marriage that is abundantly more than you can think or ask. He is able!

Faith-Filled Ideas

Spend some time thinking, praying, and planning about how you can add the fruits of the Holy Spirit—love, joy, peace, patience, kindness, goodness, faithfulness, gentleness, and self-control—into your marriage. Put the ideas God gives you into your planner or calendar.

Choose a 1-minute slot of time every day to stop, be still, and dedicate time to worshipping God in prayer and meditation. Devote yourself to this daily practice for 30 days. After that, try another 30 days, for perhaps 2 minutes a day. Ask a friend to join you!

journal

_____

_____

_____

_____

_____

_____

_____

_____

> **"** The LORD God said, 'It is not good for the man to be alone. **"**
> I will make a helper suitable for him.'
> ~ Genesis 2:18

"Pity the married couple who expect too much from one another."
~ Ruth Bell Graham

- It's a brand new day to spend time with Jesus! He is longing to meet with you and teach you how to love your husband well. Pray for God to give you His wisdom to help you understand today's study and apply it to your life.

- Grab your Bible and Read Genesis 2:18 and Ephesians 5:22-23. Write both of these powerful verses in your journal.

Let Your Man Lead!

By: Deb Weakly

Do you ever feel disheartened because your husband doesn't lead your family spiritually? Or maybe he does lead, but not like you think he should? Have you prayed for God to help him be more intentional with teaching your kids about spiritual things but still don't see any change?

The Bible says we women are to submit to our husbands, following their lead in our home. What do we do when we want to follow God's Word but feel held back by our husband's lack of faith and leadership?

I felt this way early in my marriage, and it caused a lot of fights between me and my husband. Eventually, the Holy Spirit began convicting me. He put His finger on my heart and made me see that I was not being held back by my husband's lack of leadership; I was being controlling and even sinful. The truth was that my expectations and standards were way too high for my poor husband to attain. I wanted a Christian home so desperately that I put unneeded pressure on my husband to perform. Instead of trusting his leadership in our home, I gave way to fear (1 Peter 3:6).

Before becoming a Christian, I made a lot of mistakes, and I was terribly afraid my children would do the same. So, I went to every parenting and mom's conference I could, looking for the perfect formula to help my husband and I to raise Christian kids who would not do the sinful things that I had done. While at these conferences, I heard the speakers say that if my husband wasn't reading the Bible to our children every single night at the dinner table, going to a men's group at church, or leading a certain way, he was falling short. Eager to be the best Christian mom I could, I tried to implement every suggestion they gave.

Poor Randy! I would come home from these conferences frustrated and disappointed in him, telling him *all* the ways he was falling short. But truthfully, he was leading; he simply led our family in *his* way, not in my way, or in the way of the "experts" I was listening to.

My husband drove us to church every Sunday, took us with him to serve as he cleaned up a yard for a single mom, and prayed with us faithfully. Randy is a man of his word who honors his commitments, the pleasant and unpleasant ones, and he taught his kids to do the same. My husband's faithfulness is quite a hard act to follow, but for some reason, all I focused on was that he wasn't reading the Bible to our kids every day.

Thankfully, God spoke to my heart and showed me that my Randy was the *perfect* dad for *our* children. He was leading them well. I finally got out of his way and let him lead!

Instead of complaining about what Randy wasn't doing, I started praying about becoming his helper. God answered this prayer by helping me find fun, simple devotions that Randy could read to our kids. I found easy devotions that I could photocopy and cut into little pieces of paper, and I put them in a jar with chocolate candy. After dinner, the kids and I loved to pick out a piece of chocolate from the jar and enjoy a yummy treat while dad read the short devotion out loud. Randy appreciated the help and soon felt like he successfully knew how to disciple our children.

I also began cooking a big breakfast on Sunday mornings, complete with bacon, eggs, and pancakes. The smell of delicious food always got our hungry kids out of bed. During breakfast, Randy would read a little devotion or a chapter of the Bible in different little voices that made the Scriptures come alive to the kids. They loved it and have fond memories of Sunday morning devotions with their daddy!

When I stopped fussing at Randy and began to help him, he began to lead more confidently. As wives, we have the ability to help our men step into their calling to be a godly husband. We need to cheer them on and be their helpers, trusting that God will work in their hearts. What a blessing it is when we get out of the way and watch God work!

Questions to Ponder
- Are there any areas in which you have unrealistic expectations for your husband? Pray and ask God to show you.

- What are some ways you can become your husband's helper? Write them down in your journal. Pray for God to help you encourage your husband instead of criticizing him.

Faith-Filled Ideas
If your husband is struggling in this area, ask him how you can help. Maybe you can help by praying for him, getting the kids ready for devotion time, and/or picking out a devotional book for him to read to the kids.

Here is a list of some of our favorites:
- *Our 24 Family Ways* by Clay Clarkson

- *Family Nights Tool Chest* by Focus on the Family Authors

- *The Picture Bible* by Iva Hoth

- *The Action Bible* by Doug Mauss

- *The Child's Story Bible* by Catherine F. Vos

Journal

Love Your Husband

> " If any of you lacks wisdom, let him ask God, who gives generously to all without reproach, and it will be given him. "
>
> ~ James 1:5 (ESV)

"If you bail out during the storms, you will miss the rainbows."
~ Anonymous

- It's time to meet with your Savior! Grab your Bible, journal, and a pen.

- Read James 1:1-8. If you have time, read the whole chapter. Pray and ask God to give you wisdom in your marriage. He wants the very best for you and your husband!

A Godly Marriage Starts with You

By: Lauraine Bailey

Marriage is hard work! The truth is that God uses marriage to sanctify us and make us more like Christ. In my own life, I see God using my marriage to transform, refine, and chisel me into the woman He wants me to be, and hopefully someone who looks more and more like Jesus as the years go by. In the area of marriage, God has taught me many things. As I prayed about what to share with you, I felt God narrowing the many lessons to a few essential, practical, daily, relevant anchors that have proven foundational in how I love the husband He has given me.

We all have seasons in which marriage is intensely and painfully hard. However, God walks with us, equipping, filling, enabling, and sustaining us. We must abide in Him and trust His sovereign goodness and character. Here are some things I do to reflect what God has taught me about marriage:

1. Daily, I pour God's Word into my soul. I have asked God to give me a passion for His Word, to make reading it a delight, and to use it to transform me and the life I live.

2. I ask God to start with me and transform me from the inside out. I cannot change another. It is not my place to be my husband's Holy Spirit. I put my blinders up and focus only on God, my relationship with Him, and the plank in my own eye (Luke 6:41).

3. I guard my heart from becoming bitter, hard, critical, self-righteous, and unforgiving according to this verse: "Above all else, guard your heart, for everything you do flows from it" (Proverbs 4:23). I daily confess any bitterness (Ephesians 4:31). When I sense bitterness or hardness of heart, I get on my face and cry out for God to cleanse me.

4. I desire to be a blessing to my husband (Proverbs 31:12). I know each husband is different, and I ask God for wisdom on how to love the husband He has chosen for me. I intercede daily for my husband. I pray for God to speak to his heart, give him wisdom, lighten his load, lead him,

and pour out His favor on him. I purpose not to tear down, belittle, bash, or criticize my husband, especially in front of my children, but to build up and honor him with my thoughts and actions.

5. I cling to God daily, walking in intimate relationship with Him. He is my refuge, best friend, counselor, comforter, healer of my wounds, hope, provider, and protector. Because I know I am accepted, pursued with a steadfast and faithful love, forgiven, and treasured, I can love my husband and others well.

If I could leave you with one last word of encouragement, it is that you and I do all of this for an audience of One. Our husband, children, friends, or extended family may never see, notice, or know all that we do or see our heart behind it. He sees. He knows. It brings Him delight when we walk with Him—loving Him, and loving those He places in our lives.

Questions to Ponder

• Am I daily in God's Word, reading, meditating, and applying what it says?

• Are my blinders up? Am I dealing with the planks in my own eyes? Am I asking God to transform me from the inside out?

• Am I attentive to the condition of my heart? Am I keeping it clean from bitterness, wrath, criticism, self-righteous judgment, unforgiveness, etc.? Am I confessing my sins and unholy attitudes? Am I dwelling on what is pure, lovely, and true?

• Am I asking God how I can bless my husband? Am I interceding daily for him? Am I building him up?

• Am I clinging to God, walking closely to Him, in constant conversation, both listening and speaking? Am I going to God first when I'm hurt, in need of counsel, or needing to be filled?

• Am I a people pleaser or a God pleaser?

Faith-Filled Ideas

On your bathroom mirror and throughout the house, write this with dry erase markers: "Live for an Audience of One." Ask your husband how you can pray for him...then pray. Study the attributes and character of God. Here are a few attributes to get you started:

• God is **good** (Psalm 25:8)

• He is **gracious** (Hebrews 4:16)

• He is **comforting** (2 Corinthians 1:3-4)

• He is **compassionate** (Exodus 34:6)

• He is **patient** (2 Peter 3:9)

• He is our **shepherd** (Psalm 23:1)

• He loves **steadfastly** (Romans 8:35, 39)

• He is **merciful** (Titus 3:5)

• He is **wise** (Romans 11:33)

• He is **faithful** (Psalm 89:18)

• He is **sovereign** (Matthew 10:29)

• He is **unchanging** (Malachi 3:6)

• He is **ever-present** (Hebrews 13:5)

journal

Food for the Soul

"Let all that you do be done in love." – 1 Corinthians 16:14

We all have a love language, and if you ask my husband what his is, he will say, "Food!" He really appreciates when I cook for him, which honestly makes me want to do it more. If your husband is like mine, and the way to his heart is through his stomach, try this recipe, and see if it's a winner. This is one of my husband's favorite recipes. It's also a great game day food and goes amazingly well with chips, salsa, and guacamole. Whatever your husband's favorite meal or treat is, go out of your way to cook it for him this week. Let him know you love and appreciate all the hard work he does for your family.

SOUTHWEST BURGERS
By: Brandi Carson

Ingredients:

1 lb. ground beef/turkey or blend

½ cup frozen corn

½ cup cooked black beans (homemade or canned), slightly mashed by hand

1 small can green chiles

½ cup finely diced red onion

2-3 tbsp. taco seasoning

Jar of your favorite taco sauce

6-8 slices of pepper jack or your favorite cheese—cheddar and colby jack work well if you want something milder

6-8 tortillas, soft taco sized

Canola nonstick cooking spray

Directions:

1. In a medium bowl, combine ground beef or turkey, corn, beans, green chiles, red onion, and taco seasoning. Gently mix well, being careful not to overwork the meat. If you are using ground turkey and the mixture seems a little wet or sticky, you can add a few tablespoons of breadcrumbs to help hold it together.

2. Preheat the grill to medium-high heat. Form 6-8 burger patties. You will want them to fit in the center of the tortilla after being grilled and be able to be fully enclosed by folding the tortilla around in a pentagon-like shape without leaving a gap. The size will depend on how large or small your tortillas are.

3. Grill on medium-high heat for a few minutes on each side until cooked through. If using ground turkey, you want to make sure your grill is well oiled before placing the patties on it or they will stick.

4. While the burgers are grilling, prep your tortillas. Lay out all the tortillas on the counter and spoon a good tablespoon of taco sauce in the center of the tortilla. Then place a slice of cheese on top of the sauce.

5. When the burger patties are cooked, place a burger on top of the cheese slice in the center of each tortilla. Then fold the sides of the tortilla around the burger in circular fashion, creating a pentagon-like shape, fully enclosing the burger in the tortilla. Turn it over and place it folded side down. Repeat with remaining burgers. When all the burgers are wrapped in the tortillas, place folded side down and spray with canola oil.

6. Turn the heat on the grill to medium to medium-low heat, and place burgers, folded side down, on grill to cook for a couple of minutes to lightly toast the tortilla. Flip and repeat. Grill on the opposite side for a couple of minutes until toasted as well. Once toasted, the tortilla usually stays in place and won't unfold. Remove from the grill.

7. Serve with sour cream, guacamole, and/or salsa.

journal

_____

_____

_____

_____

_____

_____

_____

_____

_____

_____

_____

_____

_____

_____

_____

_____

_____

_____

_____

_____

_____

_____

_____

_____

_____

_____

_____

Love Your Husband

Love Your Husband

~ Week Two ~

"'Am I only a God nearby,' declares the Lord, 'and not a God far away? Who can hide in secret places so that I cannot see them?' declares the Lord. 'Do not I fill heaven and earth?' declares the Lord."

~ Jeremiah 23:23-24

Hello Sweet Mom!

As I sit down to write about our upcoming study on loving our husbands, one thought on marriage prevails on my heart: when we say, "Yes" to Jesus, we enter into an eternal marriage covenant with Him. He loves so deeply and unconditionally, never stopping to lavish His love on us no matter how ugly, unfaithful, and unloving we are. He never says, "I'm done with you."

Jesus never ends our relationship, but rather always believes for the best, hopes for good, good things, and patiently endures all things for our sake! He sees a better end and wants everyone to know and experience His love. Once we come to know this love, nothing is impossible! We hold this power of love in our hands—to love the ugly and the unloveable like He does.

My friend, I don't know what your marriage looks like. What I do know from personal experience is that loving well takes a lot of hard work! Putting time aside to pray, hear, and share our deepest desires takes effort.

How beautiful that in all of this grueling, selfless work, Jesus shows us the way. He shows us how to serve, forgive, and minister from His heart to others. His love makes it possible for us to love our husbands well.

I'm praying for your marriage today, sweet one. Allow yourself to sit and receive the love of Jesus today. Let Him forgive, minister, and serve you as you wait to be filled. May He give you strength to dig deep into the power of His Spirit to continue on.

With Love,
Mari Jo Mast and the Help Club for Moms Team

> **"** *Your husband needs you to love him,*
> *but he also needs you to like him as a friend.* **"**
>
> ~ Emerson Eggerichs

Mom Tips

By: Leslie Leonard

"Let all that you do be done in love."
~ 1 Corinthians 16:14 (NKJV)

The Wise Woman Builds Her Spirit

- Write 1 Thessalonians 2:7-8 on your notecards or bathroom mirror. I especially like the NASB translation. Memorize the verses by the end of the week.
- Play praise and worship music in your car this week while running errands. Dig deeper by listening to the Bible on CD.

The Wise Woman Loves Her Husband

- Spend 10 minutes every morning praying Scripture over your husband.
  Here are some suggestions:

  Proverbs 18–Listen without interruptions. **James 1:19**–Speak without accusing.
  Proverbs 21:26–Give without sparing. **Colossians 1:9**–Pray without ceasing.
  Proverbs 17:1–Answer without arguing. **Ephesians 4:15**–Share without pretending.
  Philippians 2:14–Enjoy without complaint. **1 Corinthians 13:7**–Trust without wavering.
  Colossians 3:13–Forgive without punishing. **Proverbs 13:12**–Promise without forgetting.

The Wise Woman Loves Her Children

- Let your children take turns recording Micah 6:8 on your phone. Play it over and over until you all have it memorized. Celebrate your accomplishment by going to a new park, taking your kids for frozen yogurt, or going on another fun outing.

The Wise Woman Cares For Her Home

- Dust the baseboards and remove the cobwebs from the light fixtures this week. Baby wipes and used dryer sheets and make great tools to catch the dust in hard-to-reach places in your home.
- Plan an afternoon of self-care quiet time before your kids come home from school or during nap time. Make yourself a cup of tea and find a place to sit down for a few minutes. Clear your mind of all the things you need to do, and just enjoy the quiet and your hot beverage.

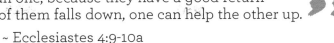

> **❝** Two are better than one, because they have a good return
> for their labor: if either of them falls down, one can help the other up. **❞**
>
> ~ Ecclesiastes 4:9-10a

"Change! If you keep doing what you're doing, you'll keep getting what you're getting."
~ Dave Ramsey

- Call your prayer partner for your 10-minute prayer call! Never underestimate the power of praying with a friend.

- When was the last time you slowed down and truly cherished your quiet time? Today, I challenge you to allow more time than you normally need, turn off your phone and any other distractions, and delve deeply into your Bible study. Let's connect with our loving Father and His boundless wisdom and mercy.

- Read Proverbs 13:11 in your Bible and write it in your journal.

Marriage & Money

By: Heather Doolittle

Regardless of your financial situation, money disagreements can put a heavy burden on any marriage. You and your husband have unique backgrounds that have shaped your individual attitudes about money. You have different fears, expectations, and goals, as well as different solutions. Ecclesiastes 4:9-10 tells us, "Two are better than one, because they have a good return for their labor: if either of them falls down, one can help the other up." It is so important to work side-by-side with your husband to hold each other accountable and balance one another's decisions, and it is even more crucial to come together to ask God to guide your decisions and bless your finances. "For where two or three gather in my name, there am I with them" (Matthew 18:20). You and your husband will reap great rewards by working together in God's counsel!

Talk to God about your money. It is an important part of your life, so He should be involved. He loves you dearly and certainly has the best plan for how to use your resources and talents wisely. He can help you utilize your gifts and stretch your finances in ways you can't imagine. Ask Him to help you and your husband agree and work together; ask Him to bless your financial decisions so you will use your money wisely. Prayer is not about manipulating God into our wills and desires or finding a way to afford all the stuff we want. It is about seeking God's perfect plan and reshaping our own plans accordingly.

> Unless the Lord builds the house, the builders labor in vain. Unless the Lord watches
> over the city, the guards stand watch in vain. (Psalm 127:1)

If we want to live in God's perfect plan for our lives, we must give God control and continually follow His direction.

All of this may sound simple in theory, but it is often easier to work with God than with your husband. With God, you have the freedom to do what you want. While it may not be wise, you can ignore God's guidance entirely and deal with the repercussions on your own. Marriage, however, does not work that way. Working with your husband requires struggle and compromise, but I encourage you to make the effort to find the solution that satisfies both of your desires. My husband and I used to discuss issues until one of us eventually gave in to the other, but we have since learned that God's plan usually lies somewhere in the middle. In discussing our finances—or any issue, for that matter—we strive to find the middle ground, and we usually find that is where God has been waiting all along.

God reminds us at least five times throughout the Bible that He created marriage for two people to come together and become one (Genesis 2:24, 1 Corinthians 6:16, Ephesians 5:31, Matthew 19:5, and Mark 10:7). Clearly, He intended to get a point across: you and your husband are more than teammates, partners, or friends. You are inseparable. You should be of the same mind and work toward the same cause, but that can only happen if you are communicating and sharing your hearts. God intended for your husband to complete you and help you become a better version of yourself, so don't undermine that purpose by neglecting to communicate and compromise.

Budgeting and saving money require years of diligence and hard work, but the end result is well worth the effort. Working in tandem with your husband will show tangible results that will increase your quality of life and lower your stress level. What better way to strengthen your marriage? After you find a way to communicate, hash through problems, and work together, your inevitable success will naturally translate into other areas of your marriage. Learning to let God lead your financial future will alleviate stress that comes from hard times. You can have peace knowing that God will bless your best, albeit imperfect, effort to follow Him and respect your husband. Just have patience. Read the Faith-Filled Idea below to learn how to get started.

Questions to Ponder

- Is God truly the head of your finances? If not, why? Ask God to help you overcome any fear or obstacle you are facing.

- Does budgeting make you or your spouse fearful or nervous? I know I have felt that way. Pray that God will help you overcome these emotions instead of avoiding budgeting altogether. Always pray before talking with your husband about finances so that tension does not rule your conversations.

Faith-Filled Ideas

Schedule a budget meeting with your husband this week. Set a day and time to review your budget. Plan accordingly (make sure you are well-rested and well-fed) and take notes on your discussion. Always pray before you begin! My husband and I plan monthly budget meetings during which we review our recent spending, tweak our budget accordingly, and discuss our financial goals. We track our savings and net worth as well. The only thing better than seeing those numbers go from negative to positive is knowing that a burst pipe or broken arm will not wreak havoc on our finances!

Gather pertinent information beforehand, plan an agenda for the meeting, and jot down short-term and long-term goals ahead of time. Do you want to pay for your children's college? Retire early? We travel more as a result of our budgeting. Once we began tracking our monthly expenditures, we realized how much more money we spend on food and miscellaneous expenses than things we love like travel and entertainment. That was all the motivation I needed to start pinching pennies at the grocery store!

Talk to your husband about starting a budget. If you are not on the same page, I suggest you join a small group through Financial Peace University. The FPU program not only forces you to come up with a financial plan in a timely manner, but it also helps you work more effectively with your spouse. I know these tasks can seem daunting, but the sooner you work out a financial plan, the sooner you'll reap the benefits from it. Start small if you must; just get started!

journal

> However, each man among you [without exception] is to love his wife as his very own self [with behavior worthy of respect and esteem, always seeking the best for her with an attitude of loving kindness], and the wife [must see to it] that she respects and delights in her husband [that she notices him and prefers him and treats him with loving concern, treasuring him, honoring him, and holding him dear].
>
> ~ Ephesians 5:33 (AMP)

"To love your spouse is to invest in blue-chip stocks."
~ Gary Chapman

- Time to grab your Bible and dig into God's Word. Read Ephesians 5:33, preferably in the Amplified version found online, and then write it in your journal.

- Do you notice that God's Word doesn't say the wife "should" respect her husband "if she wants to" or "if he deserves respect"? It says she must! Wow, let that sink in a minute. It's our job to honor and respect the man we married! If you haven't respected your husband, ask the Lord to forgive you. Share with your husband your struggles and ask for his forgiveness. Let him know how much you appreciate and respect him, despite the times you haven't shown him appreciation and respect.

Loving Your Husband

By: Rae-Ellen Sanders

When my husband and I were just married, we had our first argument the day after we got home from our honeymoon! As soon as we got home, I plopped on the couch, kicked off my shoes, and turned on the television. My husband looked at my shoes on the floor and asked me when I was going to put them away. I told him I would do it when I was done relaxing. He responded, "Why not put them away now?" Well, that's when our first spat began. I learned right from the beginning that my husband likes his home clean and, though he does not demand this from me, we work better together when we understand each other's expectations.

I have been married for sixteen years, and my house cleaning skills have improved. However, that didn't happen overnight. After the first couple of children, my husband realized we couldn't keep our place picture perfect. Five children later, I now delegate some of the housework to my kiddos, but I still do my best to please my husband in this area.

What pleases your husband? Marriage takes work. Love is a sacrificial, unselfish choice in which you put another above yourself. It is an act of will and requires personal discipline. Be encouraged in this: Christ loves your marriage and designed you to be your husband's helpmate! God helps us by giving us guidelines in Scripture, godly mentors, and wonderful Christian resources to read and study.

Recently, I read *The Five Love Languages* by Gary Chapman. It has helped me realize how I can love my husband better. Being knowledgeable of your spouse's love language and how to express love is vital in a marriage. My man's love language is words of affirmation. Although what he says is nice and flattering, his words are not my love language. Don't get me wrong, I love the accolades, but love in action—known as acts of service—blesses me more.

Chapman writes, "Your emotional love language and the language of your spouse may be as different as Chinese from English. No matter how hard you try to express your love in English, if your spouse understands only Chinese, you will never understand how to love each other."

Often, we try to fill our spouse's cup with what works best for filling our own. Although I need acts of service to make me feel loved, words of affirmation are important to my husband. So, I tell him daily how much I love him and appreciate his hard work and strong ethics. By acknowledging his positive traits, I fill my husband's cup and make him desire to be an even better provider, father, and lover. Verbal appreciation can really change the climate of a marriage!

My spouse and I openly talk about what we each do that makes the other happy, and we've discovered that our needs are different. I am sure you and your spouse are wired differently, too. Interestingly, according to Chapman, we have a primary love language and also secondary ones. Physical touch is pretty important to my husband. I am sure this is top on the list for most men. You might just find your husband has more than one love language and that you do too.

My husband now brings me coffee in bed with a good morning kiss to wake me up. Sometimes, he will run a bubble bath for me and tell the children that it's "mom time" so I can soak in peace. He has been known to buy my favorite chocolates and bring home flowers for no other reason than to show me he loves me.

Knowing that your spouse is enriched by your effort will also give you a sense of satisfaction. Your spouse will feel appreciated and be more willing to please you in your language. I highly recommend reading this book if your marriage needs a little refresher!

Questions to Ponder

Read Genesis 2:18 (NASB)

- Think about what being your husband's helper entails. How can you help him on a regular basis? Ask God for the grace to submit to your husband both outwardly and inwardly. Ask the Lord to reveal to you a few ideas, write them down, and pick one to try today!

- Consider putting his needs before your own. Reflect on how you can encourage and compliment him more.

Faith-Filled Ideas

In today's culture, we can strive to be set apart from the sinful ways of the world by earnestly loving our husbands. As mothers, the example we set when loving our husbands will impact our children and leave a legacy for future generations. Challenge yourself to love your husband with his love language and watch your marriage soar!

journal

> **"** And the Lord God said, 'It is not good that man should be alone;
> I will make him a helper comparable to him.' **"**
>
> ~ Genesis 2:18 (NKJV)

"I used to want the perfect marriage and it drove me to distraction. Because marriage is never perfect. The more I learned to find my satisfaction in God, the more satisfied I became with my husband and my marriage."
  ~ Barb Raveling

- Hello, precious woman of the Most High God. Grab your favorite beverage, your journal, a Bible, and a heart to see and hear what God has to share with you today.

- Read Genesis 2:18. Then write it in your journal as a reminder that God created you for your husband.

Loving Well through the Distance

By: Pam Mays

When God created Eve for Adam, she was meant to be his helper—the one who would walk alongside him in the garden of life. Like Eve, we have been given to our husband as his helper. But what does it mean to be a helper? What are some challenges you might face in the role of helper, especially when you are physically or spiritually apart from your husband? And what are some practical examples you can use to help cultivate and maintain a healthy marriage through times of separation?

First of all, helper doesn't mean servant. The word "helper" refers to a loving companion with whom our husbands go through life. Consider this revealing definition from an article called "A Suitable Helper" by Marg Mowczko:

> In English, the word "help" has a broad range of connotations. "Help" can refer to a simple, modest act, or it can refer to something much more vital and significant. An example of vital help is the assistance provided by doctors. In Hebrew, the word for "helper" used in Genesis 2:18 and 20 is ezer (pronounced "ay-zer"), and it is always and only used in the Old Testament in the context of vitally important and powerful acts of rescue and support.

So, ladies, we are powerful companions to our husband—sometimes our role is to support, and other times, to rescue. In marriage, our effort should be 100 percent. This applies to us as well as our mates. There will be times of imbalance, when we are exerting more effort than our husbands, but our goal should be maximum effort anyway.

When we get married, it's supposed to be for better, for richer, and for keeps, right? I can tell you that life throws curveballs that sometimes shake these assumptions. As a military spouse of 22 years, the government was responsible for most of the curveballs that came my way. In the

beginning, it was just my husband Galen and me, and we could maintain our relationship well even with distance. But when we started having kids, I had a harder time managing the household, caring for the children, and showing love to my husband. When I could devote my full attention to him, I would do sweet things like tucking a short, sweet note in his suitcase before he left for a trip. We would talk over the phone at least once a day. When we lived in California and he was at the Weapons School in Nevada, I would drive over seven hours to visit him. I made my husband my priority. His classmates teased that I visited more times than he was in class! One time, during a 6-month course, I had my in-laws watch our 4-year-old son and flew over just for dinner. I surprised him with a call and said, "What are you doing for dinner? Pick me up at the airport and let's go out!"

It's not always miles that separate you from your husband. Sometimes, it's just the busyness of life. In my case, my husband couldn't share what he did at work most of the time. On top of that, my husband is an introvert, so talking at any length with him takes a lot of warming up. In order to make some time each month to talk, we would get a babysitter for just a couple of hours, or we would trade with another family so we could talk and focus on one another.

When we lived in Georgia, there were no cute cafes or diners in our area to have a cup of tea or coffee, so we would go to the small Starbucks kiosk at our local Kroger grocery store. We had some of the best conversations in Kroger. We would often sit in the car to talk for a while after getting home from church on Sundays. These were special and sweet times.

What you do doesn't have to be elaborate. The best thing I can recommend after 23 years of marriage is to keep talking, keep being intimate, keep respecting, and keep loving. Galen and I have found that by keeping God at the center of our lives and taking the time to do things with a right heart, God has been honored and glorified, and He has helped our marriage blossom. He will do the same for you.

Questions to Ponder

• How have you handled the curveballs that life has thrown at you?

• What can you do to make meaningful connections with your husband during this season of your life?

My prayer for you:

"Dear Father, I pray that this amazing woman will be led to ideas about how to make her marriage fun and full of love. May she seek You to lead her in ways that will best fit her marriage. In Jesus' Name, Amen."

Faith-Filled Ideas

Be beautiful. When your husband returns from a trip, put on a favorite dress, fix up your hair, and apply a bit of makeup. Have the children in clean clothes with their faces washed, and if you have time, make some simple "Welcome Home, Daddy" signs. You'll be amazed at his response!

Make time to be intimate, even though it can be exhausting. When my children were young, I would faithfully schedule two days a week to be intimate with my husband. He never complained!

Try a Bible study on the topic of marriage. I did one called "Enhancing Your Marriage" by Judy Rossi. More recently, as Galen and I are geographically separated due to work, I do a nightly devotional over the phone with my him and my children. We do one with our boys first, pray with them, and then do a marriage study together. YouVersion is an excellent Bible app for countless devotions, covering every topic imaginable.

journal

journal

He is Risen

A FOURTEEN DAY LENT DEVOTIONAL FOR MOMS AND KIDS

He is Risen:

A FOURTEEN DAY LENT DEVOTIONAL FOR MOMS AND KIDS

By: Tara Davis

Resurrection Sunday is almost here! As believers, Easter is the most meaningful holiday of the year, and we have the priceless gift of sharing it with our children. In fact, the best thing we can do with our short time here on Earth is to share Jesus with these precious people God has entrusted to us! Your children are never too old or too young to be reminded daily of the message and love of Jesus! This Easter banner and devotional will be a sweet spot for you and your children to rest together in this season leading up to Resurrection Day!

Let's Get Ready!

This devotional is meant to be completed in the two weeks leading up to Easter Sunday, but feel free to start earlier and stretch out that time, just reading a few devotionals a week with your children. After planning the days you intend to set aside for this activity, there are just a couple things you will need to do to prepare.

1. **Print and assemble the banner and ornaments.** *The banner and daily ornaments can be found in coloring page format at myhelpclubformoms.com.* The whole set is super easy to construct, requiring only scissors, a bit of string or ribbon, and tape! There are detailed instructions on the printable to help you with assembly; so set aside a few minutes to put it all together!

2. **Choose a place to hang the banner in your house.** *The flags that make up this banner are actually pockets in which you will slip little daily ornaments for your kids to take out, color and hang on an Easter tree.* You will want to choose a place in your home that your kids are able to easily reach. Make sure to secure the hanging banner in a way that will stand up to little hands.

3. **Set up an Easter tree.** This is as simple as stepping outside, cutting some small twigs off a tree or bush and placing them in a jar or vase. Set your Easter tree on a table or shelf in your home. Easy! This Easter tree is where your children will hang their ornaments throughout the next couple weeks.

Daily Instructions:

The Easter banner devotional will give you a beautiful opportunity to share Jesus with your kids in the days ahead! Each day, gather your children together and then complete the following simple steps:

1. Choose a child to pull the ornament out of the Easter banner pocket for that day, or make extra copies of the ornaments so there is one for each child in the daily pocket.

2. Head to the table with the ornaments and say a quick prayer together before beginning the devotional.

3. Let your kids color the ornaments as you read the daily Scripture passage and the short daily devotional.

4. Ask your kids for their thoughts on the daily reading and then let them hang their ornament. Voila! You are done for the day!

Take it a Step Further (Optional Ideas):

- Find an Easter hymn that resonates with your heart and play it each morning as you begin your devotional time with your kids. A few suggestions are: "In Christ Alone," "How Deep the Father's Love For Us," "Jesus Paid it All," and "My Hope is Built on Nothing Less."

- Put together a prayer jar with names of people you know. Each day, let your child pull out a name and pray for that person specifically.

- Help your kids create a Jesus notebook to document the story of our Savior. Gather paper and a binder (or a spiral notebook or artist sketchbook), crayons, markers, and pencils. As you read each day, let your children illustrate the daily passage and devo in their notebook. Then, if they would like, they can write (or have you write for them) a super short summary of what they learned. Make this a fun exercise, not a chore for them. If they are not interested, don't push it. You want this to be a pleasant time of growing closer to their Savior! This is such a beautiful season in their lives!

- Check out some of our other Easter ideas throughout this book and incorporate them into your devotional time with your children!

Day 1: Prepare your heart, Pray for your child (no reading or ornament to hang)

This may seem like a day you can just skip in favor of starting the real meat of this devotional tomorrow. Don't do it! This is possibly the most important day of all. Today is a time to prepare your heart to worship your Savior with your children during these next two weeks. And it is a time to pray for the hearts of your children to know more deeply the love of God through this season and to connect with the story of Jesus in a way that will change their lives forever! What a gift today is!

Pray the following Scriptures for yourself:

- Lord, help me to draw near to you, to submit to you. Show me how to live a life of worship to you. Come near to me Lord!
- James 4:7-8 – "Submit yourselves, then, to God. Resist the devil, and he will flee from you. Come near to God and he will come near to you."
- Lord, show me how to disciple my children, how to point them to you and how to pour your love into them every day!
- Deuteronomy 6:6-7 – "These commandments that I give you today are to be on your hearts. Impress them on your children. Talk about them when you sit at home and when you walk along the road, when you lie down and when you get up."

Pray the following Scriptures for your children:

- Lord, in these coming weeks, show my children in a new and heart-changing way how great your love is for them!
- Ephesians 3:17-19 – "And I pray that you, being rooted and established in love, may have power, together with all the Lord's holy people, to grasp how wide and long and high and deep is the love of Christ, and to know this love that surpasses knowledge—that you may be filled to the measure of all the fullness of God."
- Lord, let my children call to you. Show them who you are, give them a desire to follow you all the days of their lives, and a passion to share you with others!
- Jeremiah 33:3 – "Call to me and I will answer you and tell you great and unsearchable things you do not know."

Day 2: Snake and fruit (ornament in the first blank flag)

Read: Genesis 3:1-7, Genesis 3:22-24

Discuss: Long ago, our God who created everything made a beautiful garden. Lush greens, fragrant blossoms, colorful fish and peaceful animals filled the garden. This creation was perfectly fashioned by its Creator without a single flaw. Then God lovingly made Adam and Eve to tend the garden, to walk with Him, to live in friendship with Him forever. He gave them all of the most beautiful gifts and lavished on them unending love. And in return, He asked just a single

thing: they must not eat the fruit from one certain tree in the garden. This tree, the Tree of the Knowledge of Good and Evil, would open their eyes to sin, evil, and death. God wanted to spare them the hurt that comes along with these desperately sad things because He loved His children so.

But one day, Satan, the great enemy of God, came to Eve in the form of a serpent. With his beauty and cunning lies, he tempted Eve with the fruit from the forbidden tree. He promised that the fruit would make her wise and powerful. She fell for his lies and promises, the desires of her heart pulling her away from her loving Father. Eve chose to disobey God. After she took a bite of the fruit and shared it with her husband, Adam, they realized they had made a terrible mistake. A wave of heartsickness and fear rushed over them. Sin had entered their lives. Sin had broken through God's perfect creation and with it a deathly shadow was cast over the beautiful garden. The eternal wages of sin is death and that day death entered into the world. All seemed lost. How could this ever be repaired? How could the once-perfect world, now broken by sin and death, ever be made right again?

But God, in His mercy and grace, had a plan. Just like a loving daddy who would do anything to rescue his children, God set a rescue plan into motion. A plan that would require sacrificing His most precious Son, Jesus. This plan was the thing that would make all things new, that would bring all who choose Him back into the Father's loving arms again. This rescue plan is a *Love Story* greater than all other love stories that has ever been told. And you, precious child, are at the very heart of this rescue mission.

Day 3: David (ornament in "H" flag)

Read: Acts 13:22

Discuss: A very long time ago, a man named David was born into a humble family of shepherds. But, God had a very special plan for him. He wasn't simply to be a shepherd, he was to be a mighty king! God saw that David was a boy who had amazing faith in Him and would one day become a man after God's own heart. But as much as David loved the Lord, David was imperfect. He was a sinner and did some very wrong things. But each time David sinned, his heart broke in sadness before the Lord.

Oh how David longed to follow God! He desperately needed God to rescue him and set him on the right path. You, precious child, so desperately need God too. God longs for us to have a heart like David. To know that we are sinners in need of a Savior. To know that the only One who can save us is our loving Father. Run, as David did, into the arms of the Lord. Seek His forgiveness. Seek your Savior!

God, in His perfect love, always has a perfect plan. David, though he was a sinful man, was part of the plan for God to rescue His children. You see, David's great, great, great, great grandson would be the Rescuer, our Savior, our King...God Himself. But that is a story for another day. Keep waiting, child, there are many wondrous things in store for you!

Day 4: Isaiah (ornament in first "E" flag)

Read: Isaiah 53:2-5

Discuss: Long ago, hundreds of years before Jesus was born (700 in fact!), God sent prophets to begin instructing the hearts of God's people to receive their Rescuer, the coming Messiah. One of these prophets was named Isaiah, and he loved the Lord. God revealed to Isaiah words to tell His people, prophecies of the Messiah's birth, His life and His death. These prophecies told specific details about where the Messiah would be born, how He would come into this world, how He would live, and how He would die. Would the predictions given by God ever come true?

Our loving Father knows all things, He can see forward to a time far into the future and back in time to the beginning of creation and beyond. And He knows you! He knows your heart, your thoughts, the very number of hairs on your head. And He loves you! His love for you is so great that it reaches to the stars, to the very edge of the universe and all the way back to your heart. He wants people to know that He is God. He wants people to know that Jesus is the Rescuer, literally God in the form of a human who has come to save all those who love Him.

The purpose of Isaiah's words, the prophecies given by God, was not simply to prepare people's hearts for the Rescuer. The purpose of the prophecies were to give eternal proof of God's love, of Jesus' Lordship. This proof would stretch through time all the way to today. All of the prophecies came true. These prophecies show us that God's Word can be trusted and that He has always had a plan in place to save us from eternal death. If we believe in Jesus as our Savior, we can know for certain that when we die our soul will live forever with the Lord in heaven and we will be given a new eternal body! Can you imagine how beautiful it will be? Trust in Jesus today!

Day 5: Jesus in a Manger (ornament in second blank flag)

Read: Luke 2:1-11

Discuss: The day had come. This was the beginning of a new chapter for the world, and indeed it is the most beautiful beginning that could ever have been written. Jesus, the Son of God came to earth as a baby! How the heavens rejoiced with sweet songs of angels worshipping the Lord on that night of Jesus' birth! He had come...our Rescuer, our Savior!

Did the whole earth celebrate Jesus? Not yet. Wrapped in His mother's love, Jesus looked like any other baby. But He was not just any other baby. He was a special miracle, a gift from God.

The beautiful rescue plan was still unfolding. God had a plan to defeat death, to release the grip of sin on humanity and bring eternal freedom to His beloved! Just you wait, my precious child, the best is yet to come! And just as the angels rejoiced, we have the opportunity to rejoice too! We have the opportunity today, and every day for the rest of our lives to live in worship to our KING JESUS!

Day 6: John the Baptist/ Baptising Jesus (ornament in first "I" flag)

Read: Matthew 3:13-17

Discuss: There was a special man named John the Baptist. He was the cousin of Jesus, and before he was even born, he was given a very special job. Perhaps even as John grew in his mother's womb, God whispered the plan to him...the Messiah was coming, the Rescuer of all mankind. John was the one to prepare the people's hearts to hear the Savior's message!

As John grew, God's call in his heart grew so strong that it compelled him to live whole-heartedly for God, and proclaim the message God had placed in his heart. He lived to only serve the Lord, which made him a little bit different than other people. He wasn't concerned with the way he looked, what he ate, or what people thought of him. He just wanted to serve God and proclaim the news of the Messiah to everyone who would listen! He told them of God's love, he told them to be ready for something...someone new, someone greater than any the world had ever seen. As he baptized believers, dipping them down in the peaceful river Jordan, he prayed that God would cleanse them of their sins and would bring them back into a right relationship with Him.

One day someone special stepped into the Jordan river, as a crowd was awaiting baptism. It was Jesus. This was the moment John the Baptist had been waiting for all of his life. He was face to face with Jesus, God in the flesh. Oh, what a moment that was! "Baptize Me, John" Jesus asked. Shocked, John replied, "Oh Lord, I should be baptized by YOU!" But He consented to Jesus. He longed to obey the Lord. As Jesus came up from the water, heaven burst open, and like fingers of brilliant light coming down, Jesus was bathed in the Spirit of the Lord. At that moment, the voice of the Father rang out, "This is my Son, whom I love; with Him I am well pleased." And so the journey of Salvation, the journey that led straight to the cross, began.

Day 7: The Miracle of the Fish and Loaves (ornament in first "S" flag)

Read: John 6:1-14

Discuss: One day Jesus was with his disciples when a crowd of people gathered to listen to His message. As Jesus taught, the crowd grew larger and the people grew hungrier. The disciples ran to Jesus, "We must do something Lord. The people must eat! But where will we find enough food to feed them?" Jesus had an idea!

With the disciple's help, He found a little boy who had a small lunch of fish and bread. "Will you give?" Jesus may have asked the boy. "Yes," was surely his response. With that small lunch, Jesus performed a great miracle and fed the whole crowd of 5,000 people! Fish and bread just kept coming and coming! Every tummy was full that day and every person in the crowd saw the amazing Lordship of Jesus.

God takes what we give Him and makes it so much more. What will you give Him today? Even if your gifts to Him seem small, He can take those tiny fruits in your life—your kindness, your love,

your passion for His Word—and make a huge impact on people around you. Even if you feel as if your love is as small as the flame of a birthday candle, when you shine it for Jesus, it can light the world aglow with the love of Christ!

Day 8: The Parable of the Hidden Treasure (ornament in third blank flag)
Read: Matthew 13:44-46

Discuss: Jesus liked to tell stories. His stories, called parables, taught people about God, His Kingdom, and how to follow Him. One day He was having a discussion with His disciples when He began to tell a story of hidden treasure. It went something like this...

There once was a man who came across an astonishing treasure hidden in a field. He could not believe his eyes; what a priceless treasure he had found! He was beyond excited. Since the field did not belong to him, he ran immediately to the owner and offered to purchase it for any amount. No price was too high! He was willing to give everything he had for that treasure, as he knew how valuable it was. He knew he was buying something far greater than a simple field. The treasure occupied all of his thoughts; oh what he would give for that treasure! After paying a handsome sum, he ran back to his new field and dug up the treasure and marveled at it. It was glorious, and it was worth every penny...

Jesus is just like that beautiful treasure. He is worth pursuing, He is worth any price. His goodness and love is so glorious that when we see Him for who He really is, how valuable He really is, thoughts of Him will occupy our hearts and minds every day. He wants us to choose Him, to seek Him, to give up everything we have to follow Him. Just as He gave Adam and Eve the choice of whether to choose sin, He gives us the choice of whether to choose Him. He is your greatest treasure, precious one.

Day 9: Let the Little Children Come to Him (ornament in "R" flag)
Read: Matthew 19:13-14

Discuss: One day when Jesus was teaching, large crowds of people gathered to hear His words. Parents began to shuffle close, arms around their little children, longing to see Jesus. Imagine what these loving parents were thinking as the warm Judean breeze ruffled their children's hair and birds soared above. Their one hope was that Jesus would embrace their sweet children and pray over them. Of course the disciples had taken on the task of keeping the crowd in order, making it possible for Jesus to continue His message. They rebuked the parents, telling them that Jesus was too busy for little trifles such as these.

Jesus glanced at his friends, "Let the little children come to me! Do not hold them back! The Kingdom of Heaven belongs to such as these!" Jesus placed His gentle loving hands on their little heads and prayed for them as only their Savior could. Oh how Jesus loves children, just like you! He wants you to come to Him everyday, all the time! He wants you to talk to Him. He wants to show you His amazing love for you, a love that is wider, longer, higher, and deeper than any love you have ever experienced. (Ephesians 3:14-21)!

1 Timothy 4:12 encourages, " Don't let anyone look down on you because you are young, but set an example for the believers in speech, in conduct, in love, in faith and in purity." God has a special plan for you! Run to Him, talk to Him, and let Him teach you how to live for Him in an amazing way! Children are so precious to Jesus, especially you my sweet one!

Day 10: The Last Supper (ornament in second "I" flag)

Read: John 13:1-17

Discuss: Passover had arrived! The celebration for all Jewish people was about to begin. But for Jesus, this would be the last Passover meal He would eat with His friends. He knew what was coming, that all the world's sin and pain and suffering were soon to be heaped upon his shoulders. One may think that this would make Jesus fearful or angry, but Jesus' heart was only filled with love. He knew that Judas, one of His closest friends, would betray Him that very night, turning Him over to the authorities to be arrested and crucified. But He continued to pour out love, a love that sacrificed and served even His betrayer.

As the Passover meal began, Jesus knelt before His friends and asked them to remove their sandals. He was going to wash their feet. Back in Jesus' day, people walked everywhere in sandals or even barefoot, so their feet were constantly caked with dirt and waste. Because it was such a disgusting job, it always fell to the lowliest servant in the house to wash the feet of a guest before a meal. But Jesus had the heart of a servant. He neatly arranged a wash basin and a towel and gently cleansed the filthy feet of His disciples.

The meaning of Jesus' act of servanthood was so much deeper than simply washing dirty feet. He wants to wash you clean on the inside as well. He wants to take your heart, a heart that is full of sin, and make it new, make it His. He wants you to be His child. As He finished washing the disciples' feet, He asked them if they understood what He had done for them. "I am your Lord and your Master, but also a servant. I want you to serve others as well."

Precious child, how will you serve others today? Will you tell others of Christ's love? My greatest hope for you is that you will allow Christ's love to invade your own heart, to wash over your entire being, for as long as you live.

Day 11: Jesus Arrested and the Crown of Thorns (ornament in second "S" flag)

Read: Luke 22:47-54, John 19:1-2

Discuss: From that first moment when Adam and Eve sinned, God set a plan in motion to bring them back to His heart and give them an opportunity to be His children once more. When the Passover meal had ended, Jesus and His disciples made their way to the garden of Gethsemane for the night. Jesus couldn't sleep; He only wanted to talk to His Father. Oh, how He wished there could be a different way to accomplish the rescue of His children. He knew His death would be painful and the payment for our sin would be even more so.

But His love for you is so great, precious child. He was willing to rescue you, no matter what it took, no matter how great the sacrifice. As they placed a crown of thorns on Jesus' head, they mocked and beat Him, but did he back down? Did He decide that the suffering was just too great a price to pay for your life? No. He wants you, and you are worth everything to Him. Can you believe how much God loves you? It is amazing how much Jesus endured for us, just to pay the price for our sins. He wants each person to choose Him, to be adopted as His own precious son or daughter. What a loving God is He!

Day 12: The Cross (ornament in "E" flag)

Read: Matthew 27:30-37, Matthew 27:50-54

Discuss: Oh, how our heart breaks when we read of our Savior dying. Remembering how the nails pierced His hands and feet, and how the crown of thorns pierced His brow makes our hearts flood with sadness over his death, and sadness over our sins. If only there was another way to save us that didn't involve our wonderful Jesus dying. But there was not. He gave His life for us so that we would not have to face a death that lasts forever.

As He hung on the cross, He took on all of the wrong things you have done, all of the sins ever committed throughout all history. And He replaced those sins with His forgiving love. He paid the price for our death; He purchased back our life. And all He asks of us is that we trust Him with every ounce of who we are.

As His earthly life began to fade away, He cried out, "It is finished!" The debt for our sins had been paid in full. He had made all things right again for those who would choose to follow Him. That day back in the garden of Eden, when man chose His own desires over God's love, this rescue plan had been set into motion. And now, through Jesus, it was complete. He gave everything for us. Are we willing to give everything, every part of our hearts and lives to Him? Today is the day to trust in Jesus!

Day 13: The Tomb (ornament in "N" flag)

Read: Matthew 27:57-66

Discuss: On that sad day Jesus died on the cross, His followers laid Jesus in a tomb. The cold darkness of the cave-tomb enveloped Him, and a deeper sadness seeped into the hearts of His friends. Was this the end? How could it be? Was everything Jesus claimed—about being God, about being the Rescuer—false? Tears were shed, and a huge, heavy stone was rolled in front of the cave's entrance. There was no turning back now. It seemed that everything the disciples had lived for was being left behind in that tomb.

But wait, a new light was dawning! Though Jesus had been buried, hope was unfurling in that deep darkness just like a seed planted within soft, dark soil. All joy had not been shattered, the best was yet to come! The gift of new life was unfolding and the world was about to change forever!

Can you imagine how it felt to leave Jesus' body behind that day? The disciples had no idea of what was coming next. They had no concept of the glory that lay before them. They were about to witness the greatest miracle the world had ever seen, the miracle that proves the truth of God's promises, the Lordship of our Savior and the immense love of our Father. But their hearts were breaking. They didn't realize that the story was still being written. Sometimes your heart may break too, but remember that God is still writing your story as well. Just like that day at the tomb, you can always trust God for what is ahead, for the beautiful tale He is telling with your life!

Day 14: HE IS RISEN! (ornament in last blank flag)

Read: Matthew 28:1-10, Matthew 28:18-20

Discuss: This is the day we have been waiting for! The most important day in the history of all the days that have ever existed since God created time. This is the day of our salvation! Jesus rose from the dead!! Jesus is ALIVE!!! And His life proves that He is God. His resurrection proves that we can trust who He says He is, that we can trust His promises for us. We can follow Him wherever He leads us in this life.

Jesus' love for us is so great that He gave his very life for you. And then, just as the book appeared to have ended in a pool of sadness, the story explodes off the page, straight out of the atmosphere, new life bursting forth in fireworks of His magnificent love. JESUS IS RISEN!!! He ascended into heaven and will come again! (Acts 1:10-11) What an amazing miracle! He is who He always claimed to be. He is God!

And we can spend eternity with Him! But we have to TRUST Him first. We have to accept the free gift of salvation that He offers us. He paid for our sins and gave us the opportunity for an abundant life lived in Him. The next chapter of your story is up to you precious child. What will *you* do with the gift Jesus has offered you?

Come to the Garden

Living Intentionally During
the Lenten Season . . . 15/5 Challenge

Mom Tips

By: Leslie Leonard

*"They speak of the glorious splendor of your majesty—
and I will meditate on your wonderful works." ~ Psalm 145:5*

As we prepare to go into our garden and spend time with our dear Savior, we have designed the Mom Tips to help you to live a bit more intentionally this Lenten season. Open your hearts to Jesus, and learn from His example. Spend time in Scripture and prayer, making your relationship with Him stronger.

For 30 out of the 40 days of Lent, be sure to focus on one tip in each of our four categories. Be intentional to do all of these tips during the Lenten Season. (You can catch up on the weekends).

Journal about your experience and what you are learning from the Lord.

The Wise Woman Builds Her Spirit

• Read the Bible for 30 days during the Lenten season.

The Wise Woman Loves Her Husband

• Pray for or with your husband every day for 30 Days.

The Wise Woman Loves Her Children

• Wake up *for* your kids instead of *to* your kids every morning for 30 Days.

The Wise Woman Cares For Her Home

• Let go of 30 items in your home during the season of Lent and *take* them to your favorite thrift store or local charity.

Easter

~ Week One ~

"The Lord will guide you always; he will satisfy your needs in a sun-scorched land and will strengthen your frame. You will be like a well-watered garden, like a spring whose waters never fail."

~ Isaiah 58:11

Precious Mama,

We at the Help Club for Moms feel honored that you would take the time to read our Bible study. Thank you from the bottom of our hearts, and welcome to Easter!

I love all of the beauty of Easter. The sun is usually starting to emerge from behind the clouds, and flowers are showing off their first small bits of new growth. It is a season of hope, redemption, and gratefulness.

Every day, Jesus reveals His power and immense love for us. When Jesus thinks of you, dear mama, He smiles. He is proud of you. He sees you working tirelessly. He yearns for deep closeness with you.

For the next six weeks, during the Lenten season, we are going through a wonderful time of intimacy with our Father called, **"Come to the Garden."** This experience will be filled with gentleness and quietness, revelations from Him, and powerful moments of prayer.

During "Come to the Garden," we are encouraging all moms to prayerfully consider spending intentional time in the Word of God. It's called our _15/5 Challenge_:

- **15 minutes of Bible reading a day for at least 30 days of the Lenten season.**
- **Five days a week.**
- **Six weeks total.**
- **Read the Scripture(s) and the short devotion each day.**
- **Come to the Lord in prayer.**
- **Write out your thoughts and prayers in the journal pages provided for each day.**
- **Keep track of your reading progress with the 15/5 Challenge Tracker Sheet on page 75. Friends, you are set free!**

Our team promises this experience will be one you do not regret! We recognize that this is a large commitment for a busy mom like yourself. However, throughout our own lives, we have seen the Lord work in mighty ways when we designate time with Him above other things in life.

You can do this mama! I am so excited to hear the stories of how you have been changed during "Come to the Garden." I am praying earnestly for each and every one of you.

Love and Blessings,
Rachel Jones and the Help Club for Moms Team

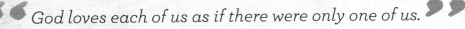

❝ *God loves each of us as if there were only one of us.* **❞**

~ St. Augustine

15/5 Challenge

__Directions:__ Color in each square as you complete it.

~ Day 1 ~	~ Day 2 ~	~ Day 3 ~	~ Day 4 ~	~ Day 5 ~
ROMANS 8:1-4	ROMANS 8:10-11	1 PETER 1:3	1 PETER 2:24	ISAIAH 53:4-5
~ Day 6 ~	~ Day 7 ~	~ Day 8 ~	~ Day 9 ~	~ Day 10 ~
1 JOHN 4:9-10	ISAIAH 53:7	ACTS 8:32	JOHN 8:28-30	JOHN 8:50-51
~ Day 11 ~	~ Day 12 ~	~ Day 13 ~	~ Day 14 ~	~ Day 15 ~
REVELATION 5:12	JOHN 1:29	JOHN 8:12, 50-51	JOHN 10:10B	JOHN 1:1-5
~ Day 16 ~	~ Day 17 ~	~ Day 18 ~	~ Day 19 ~	~ Day 20 ~
PHILIPPIANS 3:10-12	LUKE 24:46-47	MATTHEW 16:21	JOHN 12:7-8	1 CORINTHIANS 15:3-4
~ Day 21 ~	~ Day 22 ~	~ Day 23 ~	~ Day 24 ~	~ Day 25 ~
MATTHEW 21:9	JOHN 12:12-14	LUKE 23:38	MATTHEW 27:46	MARK 16:1-3
~ Day 26 ~	~ Day 27 ~	~ Day 28 ~	~ Day 29 ~	~ Day 30 ~
JOHN 20:8	MATTHEW 28:5-6	LUKE 24:5-6A	JOHN 11:25-27	1 CORINTHIANS 15:54B-55

Available as a printable at myhelpclubformoms.com!

"So now there is no condemnation for those who belong to Christ Jesus. And because you belong to him, the power of the life-giving Spirit has freed you from the power of sin that leads to death. The law of Moses was unable to save us because of the weakness of our sinful nature. So God did what the law could not do. He sent his own Son in a body like the bodies we sinners have. And in that body God declared an end to sin's control over us by giving his Son as a sacrifice for our sins. He did this so that the just requirement of the law would be fully satisfied for us, who no longer follow our sinful nature but instead follow the Spirit."

~ ROMANS 8:1-4 (NLT) ~

Friends, you are set free. You no longer live by the flesh, but you live by the Spirit because of what Jesus did on the cross! Today, we encourage you to truly live in freedom. Jesus was our sin offering, sent here by God on our behalf. Do not live under the weight of your sin another second. Live free! As you ponder Resurrection Sunday and all that it means, let the Spirit guide you, move you, and uplift you. Praying for you today, mama. May this first day of preparing your heart for Easter be a sweet one!

⇒ Journal WHAT GOD SPOKE TO ME · MY PRAYER REQUESTS

Come to the Garden

_____
_____
_____
_____
_____
_____
_____
_____
_____
_____
_____
_____
_____

And Christ lives within you, so even though your body will die because of sin, the Spirit gives you life because you have been made right with God. The Spirit of God, who raised Jesus from the dead, lives in you. And just as God raised Christ Jesus from the dead, he will give life to your mortal bodies by this same Spirit living within you.

~ ROMANS 8:10-11 (NLT) ~

The Spirit of Him who raised Christ from the dead is living in YOU! Can you believe that? It is nothing short of incredible. At any given moment, we are able to tap into that Spirit. We can ask for wisdom, guidance, direction, comfort, peace...You name it.

Today, don't forget to let the Holy Spirit lead you. Jesus speaks directly to your heart through the Holy Spirit. Pray, ponder, and meditate on the words you have read in the Bible. Let His Spirit bring you life and renewal today!

Journal — WHAT GOD SPOKE TO ME · MY PRAYER REQUESTS

Blessed be the God and Father of our Lord Jesus Christ! According to his great mercy, he has caused us to be born again to a living hope through the resurrection of Jesus Christ from the dead.

~ 1 PETER 1:3 (ESV) ~

Praise God from whom all blessings flow! He is the picture of mercy. His light shines on us each and every day because of His death on the cross and resurrection! Spend a few moments today praising Him. Turn up the worship music! Dance in your living room! Tell someone about Him and be filled with His great love for you today, mama.

Journal — WHAT GOD SPOKE TO ME · MY PRAYER REQUESTS

_____
_____
_____
_____
_____
_____
_____
_____
_____
_____
_____
_____
_____
_____
_____
_____
_____
_____
_____

Come to the Garden (side tab)

"He himself bore our sins' in his body on the cross, so that we might die to sins and live for righteousness; 'by his wounds you have been healed.'

~ 1 PETER 2:24 ~

By His wounds we are healed. What a treasure! Jesus paved a new way for us. He broke through the sin barrier that separated us from God and made a way for us. You are empowered today by Christ to live in righteousness and faithfulness in response to His love. You are able to live healed, forgiven, and redeemed through Him who is able to save and restore! Take in all that goodness today, friend. Because it truly is so, SO good!

Journal • WHAT GOD SPOKE TO ME • MY PRAYER REQUESTS

_____
_____
_____
_____
_____
_____
_____
_____
_____
_____
_____
_____
_____
_____
_____
_____

"*Surely he took up our pain and bore our suffering, yet we considered him punished by God, stricken by him, and afflicted. But he was pierced for our transgressions, he was crushed for our iniquities; the punishment that brought us peace was on him, and by his wounds we are healed.*"

~ ISAIAH 53:4-5 ~

Jesus took our pain and bore our suffering on the cross so we wouldn't have to. What a gracious gift! This is something that is easily taken for granted in our day-to-day Christian walk. Take some time today to thank Jesus for bearing your pain. Thank Him for the gift of your salvation. Thank Him for offering himself when He didn't have to.

Allow your praise and gratefulness to turn into joy. Choose to live joyfully and free today, mama! We have completed the first week of Lent! We pray your heart has been drawn closer to Jesus this week. Hugs to you!

Journal ~ WHAT GOD SPOKE TO ME · MY PRAYER REQUESTS

_____

_____

_____

_____

_____

_____

_____

_____

_____

_____

_____

_____

_____

_____

_____

My Character House

By: Tara Davis

"Therefore be imitators of God, as beloved children."
~ Ephesians 5:1

Our character is like a house that we live in. We must choose to intentionally build our character, one board at a time. We can trust our Savior Jesus, who is the Master Builder, to guide us each step of the way. And when we have Him as our foundation, our house is built on solid ground!

A character home that is well built and taken care of is a comfortable place to live and welcomes others in with the light of Jesus. However, it is easy to destroy our character house. Each time we choose to do the wrong thing, we tear apart our house one board at a time, leaving us with a home that is untrustworthy and in shambles. Trust God to help you intentionally build your character house today. Allow Him to be your foundation and your guide!

Directions:

1. Print out a character house sheet, as seen on page 82, for your child from myhelpclubformoms.com
2. Brainstorm the character qualities your child would like to be intentional about building.
3. Write those qualities on the boards of the home. Help your child brainstorm situations that would build these character qualities in them and conversely, situations in which your child would be tearing down their character house.
4. Pray with your child and ask the Lord to be their foundation and guide them in the way they should go.

My Character House

For no man can lay a foundation other than the one which is laid, which is Jesus Christ. 1 Cor. 3:11

I love rich and creamy cream cheese frosting! I can get lost in it, like the old Calgon commercials where a bath just took you to another place! Of course, there is no better combo, in my opinion, than moist carrot cake and heavenly cream cheese frosting! This 2-layer beauty has become a tradition at our table every Easter/Resurrection Sunday. I hope you enjoy it too!

This recipe is super easy unless you go old school and grate your own carrots. I did this once and not only did the carrots turn my fingers orange, but also, it took a really long time to grate a 3 pound bag! I will tell you that I did feel *extra* accomplished after it came out gorgeous and unbelievably rich!

Note: Fresh shredded carrots contain far more water than store-bought shredded carrots. However, if you add just one tablespoon of water and let them soak a bit before folding them into the batter, this cake will still impress! Also, I believe that the type of vanilla you use makes a huge difference! If you want ordinary frosting, use ordinary vanilla. *If* you want out of this world frosting—invest in a Madagascar Vanilla Extract or a Pure Bourbon Vanilla like the one I use from Trader Joe's. I also believe your cinnamon needs to be high quality. Spices are not all created equal. Your taste buds will thank you for the upgrade!

SUPER SUCCULENT SPRING CARROT CAKE

By: Rae-Ellen Sanders

Ingredients:

2 cups flour (I use all-purpose white flour, but feel free to use gluten-free)

2 cups sugar

2 ½ tsp. cinnamon

½ tsp. nutmeg

2 tsp. baking soda

1 tsp. salt

1 ½ cups vegetable oil

3 cups shredded carrots

1 tablespoon water (if using packaged shredded carrots)

4 eggs

2 tsp. vanilla (the good stuff!)

Directions:

1. Start with your flour and sugar, and sift! Yep, you read correctly—sift! I promise it is worth the time to do this! If you don't have one of those cool sifting devices like your grandma had—simply take a stainless steel mesh colander and start shaking your flour and sugar through it into a large mixing bowl. This makes your flour and sugar really fine.

2. Add the remaining dry ingredients.

3. Slowly add the oil, whisking fervently until well blended. It might seem like this is way too much oil, but trust me, it is the secret to how moist and delicious this cake is! This may be your only workout until the fork-to-plate action that will take place later!

4. Place 3 cups of the shredded carrots into the food processor and chop to a fine texture. Increase liquid by adding 1 tablespoon of water to soak. Don't drain!

5. Using a hand mixer, mix the eggs and vanilla into the batter.

6. Next, combine your carrots and fold it all in. Voila!

7. Pour the batter into two prepared greased cake pans of the same size.
   Tip: Use wax paper cut to fit inside your pans for an easy release.

8. Bake at 350 degrees for 40-45 minutes.

9. Test with a good ol' toothpick or fork to make sure it comes out clean.

10. Let cool completely before frosting.

Now for the terribly, irresistibly creamy cream cheese frosting! I have a few extra tips for you here. Soften the cream cheese and butter by placing them in a bowl on your counter before you start mixing your cake batter. Do not microwave to soften. I am opinionated on brand here as well. Philadelphia Cream Cheese blends more easily than other varieties. Very importantly, make sure to use full-fat butter, not margarine. I have doubled this frosting recipe because you will apply a nice, thick layer between the cakes and a generous layer on top. If you think it is too much frosting, feel free to cut the ingredients in half. You are creating greatness here—so don't worry about the calories until you are on your second piece!

HEAVENLY CREAM CHEESE FROSTING

Ingredients:

2 cream cheese bars (16 oz.), softened

1 stick of butter (½ cup), softened

4 tsp. vanilla

2 lbs. powdered sugar

2 tablespoons milk

Directions:

1. Using a hand mixer, blend the cream cheese, butter, and vanilla together. Slowly add in the powdered sugar until thick and creamy. Add milk as needed for desired texture. This is sweet but it compliments the carrot cake perfectly!

2. I always do a crumb layer first, which is spreading enough frosting around the tops and sides of both cakes to hold down any crumbs.

3. Place in fridge or freezer for 20 minutes to set.

4. Take out and place the bottom layer on a special plate or cake platter. Add a good amount of frosting to create a yummy middle layer and top with the other cake.

5. Frost the sides and top. Decorate with shelled and chopped walnuts or pecans pressed into the sides (optional). Indulge!

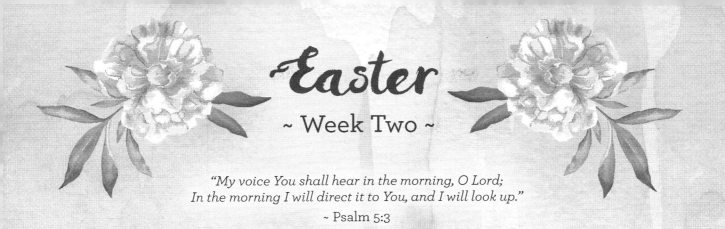

Easter
~ Week Two ~

"My voice You shall hear in the morning, O Lord;
In the morning I will direct it to You, and I will look up."
~ Psalm 5:3

Dear Mama,

How does your garden grow? I love this "Come to the Garden" theme for Lent. Coming before the Lord in Bible reading, prayer, and journaling 15 minutes a day for five days is a sure way to cultivate our relationships with Jesus! How did your first week go? Did you use the journal pages to reflect what the Scripture spoke to your heart? Here at the Help Club for Moms, we hope you get the most out of the time you set aside to listen to God and to hear His still, small voice. This invitation to the garden is meant to slow us busy mamas down so we can reflect on the true meaning of Easter: redemption of sin through Christ's death on the cross, His glorious resurrection, and ascension to sit at the right hand of the Father. Victory!

Often believers will give up a pleasure during Lent to identify with Jesus and His suffering. We encourage you to sacrifice some of your time each morning to do the 15/5 Challenge with a renewed passion to be in the Lord's presence. I promise He will meet you! Allow the Holy Spirit to till the soil of your heart and prune/correct areas in your life that need alignment with God's Word over the next five weeks. New growth is what spring is all about! If you enjoy the scent of flowers, light a floral candle while you have your devotions each morning, and it will enhance your time in the garden.

With love,
Rae-Ellen Sanders and the Help Club for Moms Team

> **"** *The sacred moments, the moments of miracle, are often the*
> *everyday moments, the moments which, if we do not look with more*
> *than our eyes or listen with more than our ears reveal only...*
> *a gardener, a stranger coming down the road behind us, a meal like*
> *any other meal. But if we look with our hearts, if we listen with all*
> *our being and imagination...What we may see is Jesus himself.* **"**
> ~ Frederick Buechner

"This is how God showed his love among us: He sent his one and only Son into the world that we might live through him. This is love: not that we loved God, but that he loved us and sent his Son as an atoning sacrifice for our sins. **"**

~ 1 JOHN 4:9-10 ~

God *is* love. He sent his Son for us so that we could know this marvelous love. As the payment for our sins on the cross, Jesus was the most beautiful example of perfect love. We can choose each day to let Christ reign in our hearts and make His love complete in us. We can choose to let this love manifest itself in us and choose to allow Him to mold us and use us for His purposes. Sweet mama, may Christ's love rule and manifest itself in your heart today!

Journal

WHAT GOD SPOKE TO ME · MY PRAYER REQUESTS

_____

_____

_____

_____

_____

_____

_____

_____

_____

_____

_____

_____

_____

_____

_____

_____

Come to the Garden

He was oppressed and He was afflicted, Yet He opened not His mouth; He was led as a lamb to the slaughter, and as a sheep before its shearers is silent, So He opened not His mouth.

~ ISAIAH 53:7 (NKJV) ~

As Jesus paid the penalty for our sins, He never complained. The Bible says, "He did not open his mouth" (Isaiah 53:7). God has shown us such great mercy! Not only was He willing to die for us, but He did it in love. This is a love unlike any we have ever known. As you let those thoughts swirl around in your mind today, remember that the same love lives in you. Let it penetrate the deepest places in your heart. Receive others with that same kind of grace!

Journal · WHAT GOD SPOKE TO ME · MY PRAYER REQUESTS

Now the passage of the Scripture that he was reading was this: 'Like a sheep he was led to the slaughter and like a lamb before its shearer is silent, so he opens not his mouth.'

~ A C T S   8 : 3 2   (ESV) ~

"Like a sheep he was led to the slaughter..." these words pierce the heart. What Jesus did on the cross was such a heavy burden to carry on our behalf. Today we are praying for God to "open the eyes of our hearts" so that we can truly feel the magnitude of what He did for us. When we take the time to imagine what it must have been like for Him, the only natural response we can have is to praise and worship Him! If you have a second today, go online or wherever you listen to music, and listen to the song *Revelation Song* by Kari Jobe. It will bless you today!

Journal · WHAT GOD SPOKE TO ME · MY PRAYER REQUESTS

_____
_____
_____
_____
_____
_____
_____
_____
_____
_____
_____
_____
_____
_____
_____
_____
_____

"So Jesus said, 'When you have lifted up the Son of Man on the cross, then you will understand that I AM he. I do nothing on my own but say only what the Father taught me. And the one who sent me is with me—he has not deserted me. For I always do what pleases him.' Then many who heard him say these things believed in him.

~ JOHN 8:28-30 (NLT) ~

As we ponder the words of Jesus from the verses above, what really stood out was "I always do what pleases Him." Mama, what can you do today that would please God? Is it an attitude change, a sacrifice He has laid on your heart, or a way that you can serve someone? Be faithful today by doing what God laid on your heart and your act of pleasing God will be a sweet aroma to Him, who loves you so dearly!

⟩ Journal ⟨ WHAT GOD SPOKE TO ME · MY PRAYER REQUESTS

_____

_____

_____

_____

_____

_____

_____

_____

_____

_____

_____

_____

_____

_____

_____

_____

And though I have no wish to glorify myself, God is going to glorify me. He is the true judge. I tell you the truth, anyone who obeys my teaching will never die!

~ JOHN 8:50-51 (NLT) ~

Jesus took away the sting of death. To believe in Him and to believe in His words in the Bible is to receive an eternal commitment from Him to enter heaven—our forever home—once we die! What an undeserved gift! We are truly blessed, friends.

Journal · WHAT GOD SPOKE TO ME · MY PRAYER REQUESTS

Tell Me Who I am in Christ!

Tell Me Who God Is!

for Kids

By: Tara Davis

As moms, we occasionally struggle with finding our identity in the world around us rather than in Christ. It is easy to forget that our kids may struggle with this concept from time to time as well. Here is a simple conversation you can have with your kids to help them remember who they really are!

Go through the following short devotion together, talk about the printables on the next two pages, look up some of the verses provided, and let your kids share their hearts with you. Hang these Scripture printables somewhere visible to remind your kids of their true identities in Christ! You can print them from myhelpclubformoms.com

Discussion:

- Hey you! Can I ask you a question? Who are you? No, not your name, silly; who are YOU?! What defines who you are? Finding out who you are—your true identity—starts with finding out more about your Creator.

- You see, you were made as an image-bearer of your Creator—you were made to look like Him, act like Him, talk like Him, live like Him. HE alone is your identity. Sometimes it's tempting to base our feelings about ourselves on what other people say about us, or on how we think about ourselves, or even how we compare ourselves to others. These are all the wrong markers of our true self though. Our identities are found solely in Jesus!

- He has made you with a purpose, and He has an incredible plan for your life! Check out this list of qualities, on page 93, that God has created you to imitate. As a kid who follows Christ, this is your true identity, and no one can take that away from you! No one knows you as God does. Listen to Him and let the way He sees you form your thoughts about yourself. Walk closely with Him as He guides you on the path He has for your life!

- When you compare these two lists of qualities, do you see how amazing your Savior is and how His qualities are reflected in His plan for you as His creation? Walk in your true identity today! Your Heavenly Father loves you SO MUCH!

Tell Me Who God Is!

for Kids

God is the Creator of all things. Nothing would exist without Him. He is worthy of all glory and praise! (Revelation 4:11)

God is the brilliant light of the world, whoever follows Him steps out of darkness and into His beautiful light! (John 8:12)

God is love! When we allow Him to live in us, He enables us to love others too! (1 John 4:16)

God is the author of all new things. Follow Him, He is writing a beautiful story in your life! (Isaiah 43:18–19)

God is perfectly good. We are blessed to trust in Him! (Psalm 34:8)

God is our refuge and strength. He is always with us and helps us in times of trouble! (Psalm 46:1)

God is gracious, righteous, and full of compassion! (Psalm 116:5)

God is our mighty Savior. He takes great delight in us, He quiets us with His love, He rejoices over us with singing! (Zephaniah 3:17)

Available as a printable at myhelpclubformoms.com!

Tell Me Who I am in Christ!

 I am God's beautiful creation. He knows me and loves me! (Psalm 139:13-14)

for Kids

 I am a light in this world, made to reflect the light of Jesus to everyone around me! (Matthew 5:14)

 I am a beloved child of God and am precious to Him! (1 John 3:1)

 I am a citizen of heaven; this world is not my home! (Philippians 3:20)

 I have an amazing purpose given to me by God. He will stengthen me to do what He has called me to do! (Ephesians 2:10)

 I can do all things through Christ who gives me strength! (Philippians 4:13)

 I was made to reflect the image of God. My ability to treat others with love and kindness comes from Him! (Genesis 1:27)

 I was chosen by God, and I am special to Him! (1 Peter 2:9)

Available as a printable at myhelpclubformoms.com!

Come to the Garden

Easter

~ Week Three ~

"...Joy and gladness will be found in her,
thanksgiving and the sound of singing."
~ Isaiah 51:3b

Dear Friends,

I hope that you are enjoying "Come to the Garden." Easter is such a special time of year. Followers of Christ around the nation and the world celebrate our risen Savior on Easter. What a fantastic reason to celebrate!!

My family celebrates Resurrection Sunday several ways. We read the Bible and Easter-themed books, decorate sugar cookies, and have a big family dinner. We take time to recognize the ultimate gift our Savior Jesus Christ gave us: eternal life with no strings attached. I know that I find this gift that was so freely given overwhelming at times.

What does your family do that is special during Easter?

I love how we are focusing on caring for our spiritual gardens during this very special time. How is your garden coming along? Are you taking the time to care for all areas of your garden? Martin Luther once said, "Our Lord has written the promise of resurrection, not in books alone but in every leaf of springtime." Take a moment to look at the budding trees and plants. Can you see the beauty all around you? I pray that you take the time to nurture and care for yourself during this Lenten season. Spend extra time praying and meditating over the words of the Bible. I know that I am making this a priority during this busy season.

I am so happy you decided to join us this Lenten season. He is risen!!

Love,
Leslie Leonard and the Help Club for Moms Team

66 *Easter is the demonstration of God*
that life is essentially spiritual and timeless. **99**
~ Charles M. Crowe

"Saying with a loud voice: 'Worthy is the Lamb who was slain to receive power and riches and wisdom, and strength and honor and glory and blessing!'"

~ REVELATION 5:12 (NKJV) ~

Even at Jesus' lowest point—death on a cross—He was exalted! The angels were singing about His power, wealth, wisdom, strength, honor, glory, and praise! It's astonishing that even in His death, His mighty power was shown. Humble yourself before Jesus today, friend. He is the one who made you and knows you. He is our hope because of what He did for us. You are so loved!

Journal · WHAT GOD SPOKE TO ME · MY PRAYER REQUESTS

"The next day John saw Jesus coming toward him, and said, 'Behold! The Lamb of God who takes away the sin of the world!'

~ J O H N 1 : 2 9 (NKJV) ~

Jesus came to take away the sin of the world. We are not saved because of what we have done, but because of what He did for us. In this verse, John is proclaiming that Jesus is the ONE who has come for us. He was so bold and brave in His faith. Today as you ponder the idea that Christ came for your sin, practice being bold as an act of gratitude. Has God been tugging at your heart to share His Good News with someone? Or maybe you need to pray about who God has in your life that He wants you to minister to?

Journal WHAT GOD SPOKE TO ME · MY PRAYER REQUESTS

Jesus spoke to the people once more and said, 'I am the light of the world. If you follow me, you won't have to walk in darkness, because you will have the light that leads to life... And though I have no wish to glorify myself, God is going to glorify me. He is the true judge. I tell you the truth, anyone who obeys my teaching will never die!'

~ JOHN 8:12, 50-51 (NLT) ~

We can all walk through times of darkness in our lives. Maybe it was before you encountered Jesus or maybe it is a trial you are currently facing in your life, but to know Jesus and to obey Jesus is to walk in the light. No matter what we are going through, if we stick close to Jesus, He will guide us and illuminate the way. His light, warmth, and presence will be the fuel that keeps us going. We needn't even fear death because He has conquered the grave! There is so much peace to be found as we follow Jesus!

⇒ Journal ⇐ WHAT GOD SPOKE TO ME · MY PRAYER REQUESTS

_____

_____

_____

_____

_____

_____

_____

_____

_____

_____

_____

_____

_____

_____

_____

_____

I have come that they may have life, and have it to the full.

~ JOHN 10:10b ~

What does it mean to "have life to the full?" It is what Jesus intended for us here on earth; it's why He came. Part of it may be finding the beauty in the mundane—noticing and feeling God's presence in the ebb and flow of life. Today's verse says, "the thief comes only to steal and kill and destroy." We can be so easily swayed by the enemy. Ask God to have His way in you—His way brings life! Take in God's goodness today and feel His life-giving joy inside your heart as you come to know and love Him more!

journal WHAT GOD SPOKE TO ME • MY PRAYER REQUESTS

_____
_____
_____
_____
_____
_____
_____
_____
_____
_____
_____
_____
_____
_____
_____
_____
_____

"In the beginning was the Word, and the Word was with God, and the Word was God. He was with God in the beginning. Through him all things were made; without him nothing was made that has been made. In him was life, and that life was the light of all mankind. The light shines in the darkness, and the darkness has not overcome it."

~ JOHN 1:1-5 ~

In this short passage of Scripture, God is directing us to His book (the Bible) as the story of God in the world, not just the story of one character in one place and time. He was, is, and always will be. He is the Word made flesh. All of creation is alive because the Word of God breathed life into it. The Word of God breathed life into us too! When people hear God's words, it changes them from the inside out. That happens because He knitted us together and knows our innermost being! Who He is penetrates the deepest places of our hearts. Nothing escapes God's view, and His Word will stand until the end of time. Our hearts can take comfort in knowing that darkness can never overcome the light of Jesus. It is too bright and powerful!

Come to the Garden (side text)

⁓ Journal ⁓ WHAT GOD SPOKE TO ME · MY PRAYER REQUESTS

_____
_____
_____
_____
_____
_____
_____
_____
_____
_____
_____
_____
_____
_____

Food for the Soul

"He is not here; he has risen, just as he said.
Come and see the place where he lay" ~ Matthew 28:6

Here is a fun and tangible way to teach your children about the resurrection. These are a wonderful treat for Easter Saturday or Resurrection Sunday.

RESURRECTION ROLLS

By: Jennifer Valdois

Ingredients:

1 can of 8 crescent rolls

8 large marshmallows

½ stick of butter, melted

2 Tbsp. sugar

1 tsp. cinnamon

Directions:

1. Preheat the oven to 375 degrees.

2. Read John 19:38-42 to your children. Explain to them what each ingredient represents.
   - The marshmallow represents Jesus, white and pure because He was without sin.
   - The crescent dough represents the linen cloth they wrapped Jesus in.
   - The butter is like the embalming oils.
   - The cinnamon and sugar are like the spices they used to prepare His body for burial.

3. Spread out the crescent dough according to package directions. Melt the butter. Mix the cinnamon and sugar in a shallow bowl. Dip a marshmallow in the butter. Roll it in the cinnamon and sugar mixture. Place the marshmallow in the triangle of dough and wrap the marshmallow completely. Pinch the dough to make sure it is sealed. Dip it in the butter again to keep it from sticking to the pan.

4. Place the rolls in a muffin tin. Put the rolls in the oven, which represents the tomb, and bake for 11-13 minutes.

5. While they are baking, read John 20:1-18.

6. Open the tomb, and immediately remove the rolls from the pan to prevent them from sticking to the pan.

7. When they are cool, let your children discover what happened to the marshmallows.

Jesus is risen! He is risen, indeed!

Easter
~ Week Four ~

"The weapons we fight with are not the weapons of the world.
On the contrary, they have divine power to demolish strongholds.
We demolish arguments and every pretension that sets itself up
against the knowledge of God, and we take captive
every thought to make it obedient to Christ."
~ 2 Corinthians 10:4-5

Dear Sister,

If you're fighting a personal battle right now, Jesus wants to bring heaven's peace into your situation and calm your raging emotions. Oh, friend, you don't have to wait until the battle is over to find peace. All can be well with your soul right now.

Maybe you think after the trial, after the storm is over, the possibility of peace becomes available. But no, Jesus actually delivers peace in the *present* (in the middle of the mess) if we can believe it. He is I AM.

Jesus said in John 16:33, "These things I have spoken to you, so that in Me you may have peace. In the world you have tribulation, but take courage; I have overcome the world."

Every battle we encounter is not between God and Satan anymore (the enemy was defeated when Jesus rose from the grave), but is an attack against the truth of God's Word, against us—a battering ram in our mind against the knowledge that Jesus was already victorious *for us*. It's so important we know and *stand* with Him on this truth because Satan wants us to believe the battle we face hasn't been won.

We overcome the lies, in the heat of the battle, and usher in peace when we keep our hearts and minds focused on Christ's finished work. Jesus is LORD; He is Lord above our struggle, over every stinking battle we encounter! The enemy is under the feet of Jesus and we are seated with Him in heavenly places.

"For he raised us from the dead along with Christ and seated us with him in the heavenly realms because we are united with Christ Jesus" (Ephesians 2:6 NLT).

Worshipping Jesus in truth brings our thoughts, emotions, and feelings under submission, into God's greater reality—IT IS FINISHED! This brings true peace.

I'm praying for you to feel calm and declare victory no matter how intense your battle is right now. Begin by agreeing with Jesus. He already overcame and He loves you! Worship Him! He is the Prince of Peace who is always available to minister in a tangible way. Ask for the Holy Spirit's help. He brings strength to sing songs of praise in the darkest night.

With love,
Mari Jo Mast and the Help Club for Moms Team

"That I may know Him and the power of His resurrection, and the fellowship of His sufferings, being conformed to His death, if, by any means, I may attain to the resurrection from the dead."

~ PHILIPPIANS 3:10-12 (NKJV) ~

The goal of the Christian life is to know Christ! We come to know God through Jesus and His Word, which tells us all about Him. Do you make time to spend with Jesus, dive into His Word, and experience "the power of His resurrection" that the verse talks about today? Understanding the power that comes through Jesus' resurrection is what sustains us as believers to abide in Him and to stay the course in our Christian walks! May you abide in Him and the power of His resurrection today, sweet mama!

Come to the Garden

➳ Journal ➳ WHAT GOD SPOKE TO ME • MY PRAYER REQUESTS

_____
_____
_____
_____
_____
_____
_____
_____
_____
_____
_____
_____
_____
_____
_____
_____

"Then He said to them, 'Thus it is written, and thus it was necessary for the Christ to suffer and to rise from the dead the third day, and that repentance and remission of sins should be preached in His name to all nations, beginning at Jerusalem.'"

~ LUKE 24:46-47 (NKJV) ~

Our verse today is an affirmation of a few things: that the Scriptures are true, that Christ must suffer, that He must rise on the third day, that all should know that their sins can be forgiven, and that we (His followers and believers) are to bear witness of these things! This is our message, friends! It is simple, yet profound—powerful, yet humble. After Jesus died for us on the cross, He asked us to go preach His name and make disciples of all nations!

As you ponder this verse today, pray about how Jesus would make this come alive in your heart and how you can apply this to your life! Ask boldly, and respond when He tugs on your heart. Our faithfulness to His promptings is what makes our faith grow.

Journal   WHAT GOD SPOKE TO ME · MY PRAYER REQUESTS

"From that time Jesus began to show to His disciples that He must go to Jerusalem, and suffer many things from the elders and chief priests and scribes, and be killed, and be raised the third day.

~ MATTHEW 16:21 (NKJV) ~

What stands out about this verse today is that Jesus wore a heavy burden. Each day leading up to His resurrection, He knew. He knew it would be so painful, that He would suffer and eventually die. I can't imagine living with this weight every day! It's unfathomable. At any time He could have decided to pass the cup, to refuse to bear the burden, and to let us suffer the price for our own sinfulness. However, we serve a gracious God! He knew the only way for us to be with Him was for Him to suffer along this road and to rise in victory proclaiming He was the one true God.

Are you having a hard time today, mama? Are you suffering in some way? Stay the course. Jesus' life was a living, breathing example to us. Story after story is written in God's Word to encourage us to have perseverance, even when it's hard. Take courage today!

Journal ~ WHAT GOD SPOKE TO ME · MY PRAYER REQUESTS

_____
_____
_____
_____
_____
_____
_____
_____
_____
_____
_____
_____

"But Jesus said, 'Let her alone; she has kept this for the day of My burial. For the poor you have with you always, but Me you do not have always.'

~ JOHN 12:7-8 (NKJV) ~

Without going into great detail, you should know that the perfume this verse is talking about was very expensive! This woman wanted to give Jesus her very best. Some scoffers thought the woman wasn't being frugal and should have helped the poor instead of lavishing love on Jesus with the expensive perfume. They thought that helping the poor was a bigger and better act of service to display to Jesus. But that wasn't the case! Jesus looked at her gift for what it was; she was giving Him all she had. He was worth that and more to her, and that is what she wanted to show her God! This Scripture is absolutely beautiful. It begs the question though...What is your best for Jesus?

Journal · WHAT GOD SPOKE TO ME · MY PRAYER REQUESTS

"For I delivered to you first of all that which I also received: that Christ died for our sins according to the Scriptures, and that He was buried, and that He rose again the third day according to the Scriptures.

~ 1 CORINTHIANS 15:3-4 (NKJV) ~

"According to the Scriptures".... two times in our verses today this phrase was written. Friends, we can *trust* the Scriptures! From the Old Testament to the New Testament, the Holy Spirit inspired the authors to write about His death and resurrection, among many other things, and each and every prophecy was fulfilled! Let your hearts be encouraged today that God's Word is trustworthy, that you too can live "according to the Scriptures!" When you read a verse, let it sink into the deepest crevices of your heart because it is truth!

Journal ~ WHAT GOD SPOKE TO ME · MY PRAYER REQUESTS

_____
_____
_____
_____
_____
_____
_____
_____
_____
_____
_____
_____
_____
_____

Palm Sunday Fun!

for Kids

By: Tara Davis

Palm Sunday is this weekend, and with it, we enter into Easter week! Palm Sunday is a perfect opportunity to be intentional about helping our children prepare their hearts for the true celebration of Easter. It's not all about the eggs, bunnies, and Honey Baked Ham! The more we can encourage our children to turn their eyes away from the world and focus on Jesus, the better. Let's do this, mamas!

This activity is primarily geared toward younger children, but check out the activities for older kids on the next page.

MAKE! — Grab some green construction paper or green paint and let's get busy. First, trace your child's hand on the green paper or alternately paint his hand with green paint and press a painted handprint onto the paper. Cut these handprints out and glue to popsicle sticks or even regular sticks from your yard. These are your palm branches.

READ! — Gather your children and read the biblical account of Palm Sunday either from your favorite children's Bible or from Matthew 21:1-11 or John 12:12-18.

LISTEN! — Dance to "Give me Oil in My Lamp" (especially the chorus). You can find it on YouTube here: (http://bit.ly/2nLvav).

PLAY! — Now it is your turn to act out Jesus' triumphal entry. Talk about the humility that is shown by Jesus. Did He ride into town on a magnificent stallion? No, He chose a donkey. He had no intention of drawing attention to himself. He was in every way a servant leader!

Sing songs of praise with your children and wave your palm branches for the King of Kings, our Savior, Jesus. Have fun worshipping the Lord together!

Palm Sunday Fun!

for Kids

OLDER KIDS ACTIVITIES:

- Older kids may enjoy a store-bought palm branch and reading through the biblical account of Palm Sunday as well.

- Ask your older kids to look at the story of Palm Sunday from the perspective of Jesus and the perspective of the crowd. Did the feelings of the crowd remain stable through Easter week? What does this teach us (Jeremiah 17:9)?

- Let your children use a creative outlet to interact with the story. Let them create a painting, a sculpture out of clay, a comic strip, a theater production, whatever suits their fancy.

- Whether you choose an activity or not, talk, talk, talk about Easter week with your older children. Allow them to ask hard questions, and be a sounding board for their faith. And pray for their hearts this week, that they would seek Jesus in an ever-deepening way!

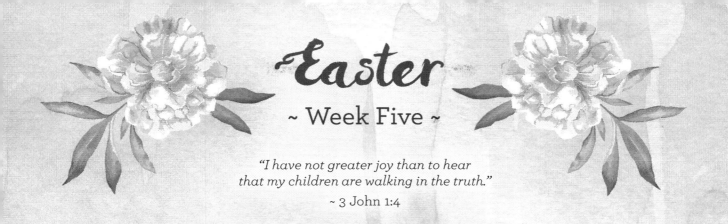

Easter

~ Week Five ~

*"I have not greater joy than to hear
that my children are walking in the truth."*

~ 3 John 1:4

Hello Sweet Mamas!

I'm so excited for Resurrection Sunday! This week, I am gathering recipes and making grocery lists. As I prepare for this meaningful holiday, this week is a time of thoughtfully considering which traditions I want to continue from my childhood and which new ones I'd like to create. Did you know that traditions are a fun, creative way to love your children well?

Traditions increase our children's sense of belonging, strengthening their feelings of support and security. They also bring about a heightened sense of family values like loyalty and trust. And, of course, they create memories and build a childhood your son or daughter can look back on fondly and use as a source of happiness.

Our family has baked homemade cinnamon rolls for Resurrection Sunday ever since I can remember. Reaching back to my own childhood, the warm smell of spices and bread rising in the oven delights me still today. It's certainly a labor of love, time, and energy. Nevertheless, I am continuing the tradition! This beautiful breakfast speaks love and blessing over my children and husband because they know how very special it is.

As we continue with week five of "Come to the Garden," my heart and soul are encouraged to love my family lavishly, whether it's with cinnamon rolls, extra hugs, or genuine smiles, because our Savior loved us first. He demonstrated an intensely sacrificial love for us by innocently dying a painful, torturous death, simply because He loves you and me that much.

So, I encourage you to find ways to start traditions and to continue old, valuable ones from years past because your family will remember, feel important, and know that you truly are the wise woman who loves them with your whole heart.

Love,
Kristi Valentine and the Help Club for Moms Team

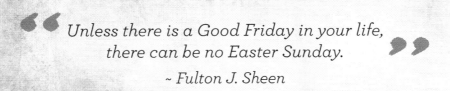

*Unless there is a Good Friday in your life,
there can be no Easter Sunday.*

~ *Fulton J. Sheen*

"Then the multitudes who went before and those who followed cried out, saying: 'Hosanna to the Son of David! Blessed is He who comes in the name of the Lord! Hosanna in the highest!'"

~ MATTHEW 21:9 (NKJV) ~

Hosanna. Do you know what this word means? Hosanna is used as an expression of adoration, praise, or joy! It was also used in praise for deliverance, or even anticipated deliverance! The people of Jesus' time knew that He was the one who came in the name of the Lord to deliver them and save them.

As you go throughout your day, use that precious word—Hosanna. Use it when you pray to Jesus today. Talk to your children about it. Make it yours! Praise Jesus for coming as your Deliverer! It may feel strange at first to utter it since it isn't a word we use often; but the meaning is rich and Jesus sees your heart. We know it will be a blessing to you today, mama!

᠈ Journal ᠈ WHAT GOD SPOKE TO ME · MY PRAYER REQUESTS

_____

_____

_____

_____

_____

_____

_____

_____

_____

_____

_____

_____

_____

"The next day a great multitude that had come to the feast, when they heard that Jesus was coming to Jerusalem, took branches of palm trees and went out to meet Him, and cried out: 'Hosanna! Blessed is He who comes in the name of the Lord! The King of Israel!' Then Jesus, when He had found a young donkey, sat on it; as it is written.

~ JOHN 12:12-14 (NKJV) ~

Earlier in the Bible, in Zechariah 9:9, it was prophesied that the king would come "righteous and victorious, lowly and riding on a donkey, on a colt, the foal of a donkey." Our verses today beg the question...Why a donkey? It is believed, for one, it fulfills the prophecy in the Old Testament (God's word is always true!), and two, rather than use a horse which was often a symbol of war in Jesus' time, lowly animals were a symbol of peace. It also connected with the poor and oppressed that He came to serve and to save!

Don't you just love that Jesus was so unpredictable? His ways were so incredibly wise and always had a deep meaning. Nothing that He did on earth was ever without thought or purpose! The verses today show us a God who was and is a peacemaker. The people expected their King to ride in on a horse and save the day, but He was lowered so we could be lifted, friends! He rode into the city bringing peace. Enjoy His peace today! His abundant peace is available to us when we simply ask.

⟩ journal ⟨ · WHAT GOD SPOKE TO ME · MY PRAYER REQUESTS

And an inscription also was written over Him in letters of Greek, Latin, and Hebrew: THIS IS THE KING OF THE JEWS.

~ LUKE 23:38 (NKJV) ~

The notice above the cross, "This is the King of the Jews," was meant to be a mockery of Jesus—to poke fun at His claims. To the believer, it prompts feelings of utter gratitude and reverence: our Savior, on a cross, dying for the sins of the world. There is no mockery in us as we ponder and surrender our hearts to Jesus for His great, undeserved love toward us! What a sweet gift it is that Jesus turned the tables. Even the words that were meant to harm Him, placed there by others, were words that He chose to put in His love letters (the Bible) to us believers. God can use all things for His glory! Jesus is King! Let your hearts be encouraged by that today! There is nothing in your life that God cannot turn around and use for His glory!

Journal WHAT GOD SPOKE TO ME · MY PRAYER REQUESTS

_____
_____
_____
_____
_____
_____
_____
_____
_____
_____
_____
_____
_____
_____
_____

Come to the Garden

About three in the afternoon Jesus cried out in a loud voice, 'Eli, Eli, lema sabachthani?' (which means 'My God, my God, why have you forsaken me?').

~ MATTHEW 27:46 ~

Even when Jesus was on the cross, He set an example of how we should live. He called out to His Father in His agony, pain, and suffering. His life exemplified the perfect model for us to go to the Father in our greatest time of need. If Jesus went to the Father, how much more should we come before God's throne in our struggles! Dearest sister, what are you carrying today that you need to bring to God and pour out to Him? What are the pains deep inside of your heart that you need to give over to your Heavenly Father? He is there for you and He will never leave you.

Journal · WHAT GOD SPOKE TO ME · MY PRAYER REQUESTS

"Now when the Sabbath was past, Mary Magdalene, Mary the mother of James, and Salome bought spices, that they might come and anoint Him. Very early in the morning, on the first day of the week, they came to the tomb when the sun had risen. And they said among themselves, 'Who will roll away the stone from the door of the tomb for us?'

~ MARK 16:1-3 (NKJV) ~

On Easter Sunday, when the devoted women in Jesus' life were on their way to the tomb to anoint His precious body with spices, they were wondering who would roll the stone away from the entrance of the tomb. Little did they know that the prophecy had been fulfilled; their Savior had risen from the dead, just as He said He would! All the prophecies of the Old Testament came to fulfillment at this moment. The Messiah, Jesus Christ, who was with God at the beginning of the world, left heaven to die a criminal's death on the cross so that you and I could be close to God. The veil was torn, there was no longer any separation between God and His children, for those of us who choose to believe. By turning our hearts to Jesus, and inviting Him to be Lord of our lives, we now have the chance to live a completely new life in Christ. Turning our eyes away from our sin and onto Jesus, we now have a whole new story and the opportunity to live eternally with Jesus in heaven. Do you know Jesus as your personal Lord and Savior? Your eternity is awaiting your decision. Will you pray with me today?

"Dear God, I know I'm a sinner, and I ask for your forgiveness. I believe Jesus Christ is Your Son. I believe that He died for my sins and that you raised Him to life. I want to trust Him as my Savior and follow Him as my Lord, from this day forward. Guide my life and help me to do Your will. I pray this in the name of Jesus. Amen."

If you prayed that prayer for the first time or if you re-dedicated your life to Jesus Christ, we would love to hear from you so we can pray for you and send you some helpful information to get you started in your new life in Christ. Please email us at info@helpclubformoms.com. For more information on becoming a Christ-follower, please go to peacewithgod.net.

ꙅ Journal ꙅ WHAT GOD SPOKE TO ME · MY PRAYER REQUESTS

_____

_____

_____

_____

_____

_____

Good Friday Breakfast!

for Kids

By: Tara Davis

Good Friday is a beautiful time for us to remember the amazing gift Jesus gave when He willingly died on the cross to rescue us from the punishment of our sin, and to offer us the opportunity to choose a life lived in Him. Would you like to do something tangible with your kids to honor our Savior and make this day more meaningful in your home? We have an idea for you!

GOOD FRIDAY BREAKFAST ACTIVITY:

- Make hot cross buns to remember the cross Jesus died on for us.
- Set the table with a nail and slip of paper at each place setting.
- Help your children make a wooden cross out of scrap wood and nails or branches and string. (Alternately, you can make a cross out of paper, even old paper bags. Keep it simple!)
- Read aloud the account of Jesus' death in Matthew 27:32-56. You could also read from a children's Bible if you have tiny kiddos.

- Ask your kids to think of a sin they struggle with and write it, with your help if necessary, on their slip of paper. Then nail or tape the slips of paper to the cross. Talk about how Jesus chose to die for those very sins with which we struggle. We do not have to be bound by those sins any longer!
- Consider the forgiveness and freedom we can find in Christ and pray together.
- If your kids would like, they can rip their papers off the cross and burn them in a glass cup or jar. When we

Good Friday Breakfast! for Kids

give our lives to Christ, He frees us from our bondage to sin. You can dip your finger in the leftover ashes and make little crosses on each child's hands. Jesus makes beautiful things from the ashes of our lives.

- Turn on some praise music, dance, and worship Jesus together!

Remember, it's okay to keep it simple. It doesn't have to be perfect to be meaningful. Sisters, it is so beautiful that we are learning how to have a Christ-focused Easter together!

Easter

~ Week Six ~

"I am the door. If anyone enters by Me,
he will be saved, and will go in and out and find pasture."

~ John 10:9 (ESV)

Dearest Mama,

As we prepare our hearts for remembering Jesus' death and resurrection, I encourage you to find quiet moments to read the Scriptures and "Come to the Garden." What a praiseworthy week lies ahead of us!

Throughout the Old Testament, a perfect spotless lamb atoned for people's sins. For every sin committed, blood needed to be shed. The Passover has such an important significance to our Easter story. The Israelites in Exodus 12:13 painted the blood of a lamb over their doorframes, so the angel of death would pass over them. Likewise, Jesus' blood covers us when we receive the free gift of salvation. The perfect sinless Son of God poured His blood out on the cross to set us free from death. He became the lamb that was slain for the sins of the world! Jesus is our Passover Lamb! He took our iniquities and the punishment we deserved and died a painful death on a tree— it is through Him that we are made clean by the forgiveness of sins. There is more good news: Satan can't touch what the blood covers. The blood of Jesus truly protects and sets us free! Hallelujah!

Jesus, who was fully Jewish, celebrated the Passover Seder, otherwise known to us as the Last Supper. The Jewish people celebrate Passover to remember the saving of their firstborn from the plague of death and their freedom from slavery. In Luke 22:19-20, Jesus announces a new covenant of His body broken for us and His blood shed, triumphing for all of eternity. As we engage in the Lord's Supper this week, take extra time to reflect on Christ's redemptive work on your behalf.

I love the correlation of the door frame in the Passover story in Exodus to Jesus Christ being the door in John 10:9, "I am the door. If anyone enters by Me, he will be saved, and will go in and out and find pasture." The entire John 10 chapter is wonderful—Jesus is our Great Shepherd who laid His life down for His sheep. I encourage you to read John 10:7-18 this week.

Praying that you have a glorious week of reverent worship as you make room for the returning King—the Messiah—to be Lord of your life!

With love,
Rae-Ellen Sanders and the Help Club for Moms Team

> *Instead of Passover pointing backward to the great sacrifice by which God had rescued his people from slavery in Egypt, this meal pointed forward to the great sacrifice by which God was to rescue his people from their ultimate slavery, from death itself and all that contributed to it (evil, corruption, and sin).*

~ N.T. Wright

Then the other disciple, who came to the tomb first, went in also; and he saw and believed.

~ JOHN 20:8 (NKJV) ~

This is just one account of Jesus' resurrection. This is the turning point in our Christian faith that sets us apart from other religions. Jesus not only died a gruesome and necessary death on the cross, but He also showed that He was the one and only God by rising from the dead on the third day. The disciple mentioned in this verse was one of the many eyewitnesses to this. It is a precious thing that Jesus inspired John to write these words to us. He wanted us to have these firsthand accounts to strengthen and solidify our faith in Him.

Knowing that we are loved by a God who humbled Himself and died for our sins is more meaningful than anything we can ever imagine. The fact that He not only wanted us to know that but even went *further* to provide proof for us who weren't able to physically see it happen, is icing on the cake. We serve such a merciful and gracious God, friends! Remember that today!

Journal · WHAT GOD SPOKE TO ME · MY PRAYER REQUESTS

_____

_____

_____

_____

_____

_____

_____

_____

_____

_____

_____

_____

_____

_____

The angel said to the women, 'Do not be afraid, for I know that you are looking for Jesus, who was crucified. He is not here; he has risen, just as he said. Come and see the place where he lay.'

~ MATTHEW 28:5-6 ~

"Fear not, for his resurrection shall be your consolation." – *Matthew Henry's Concise Commentary*

The quote by Matthew Henry above is so powerful and true! The angel in today's verses was comforting the women and telling them not to fear. To "console" means to alleviate or lessen the grief, sorrow, or disappointment. Jesus' resurrection meant there was hope! This was unlike any other death these women had experienced—there was no sting! Jesus was not gone forever. He hadn't abandoned them; it was the exact opposite! He had pardoned them and paved a way for them eternally! I cannot imagine what these two women felt, but as we look back in time at this moment, it is so powerful and filled to the brim with *hope!*

⟐ Journal ⟐ WHAT GOD SPOKE TO ME • MY PRAYER REQUESTS

_____

_____

_____

_____

_____

_____

_____

_____

_____

_____

_____

_____

_____

_____

"A nd as they were frightened and bowed their faces to the ground, the men said to them, 'Why do you seek the living among the dead? He is not here, but has risen.'"

~ LUKE 24:5-6a (ESV) ~

Reading this verse in the context of our lives today, how often do we feel hopeless in our circumstances and forget that we have Jesus living inside us, ready to help us? His death on the cross was not the end of His story! This is so easy to forget when we are overwhelmed with our lives! His death *and* resurrection are what makes it possible for us to continually lean on Him and receive His help and direction. As believers, we never need to fear or despair! Our God lives *in* us and is able to do far more than we can even imagine! Be encouraged today!

Come to the Garden

Journal · WHAT GOD SPOKE TO ME · MY PRAYER REQUESTS

_____

_____

_____

_____

_____

_____

_____

_____

_____

_____

_____

_____

_____

_____

_____

_____

"Jesus said to her, 'I am the resurrection and the life. He who believes in Me, though he may die, he shall live. And whoever lives and believes in Me shall never die. Do you believe this?' She said to Him, 'Yes, Lord, I believe that You are the Christ, the Son of God, who is to come into the world.'"

~ JOHN 11:25-27 (NKJV) ~

Jesus' message of salvation is so simple: believe in Him! We love that He says in these verses that He is the resurrection and *the life*. For those of us who have believed in Jesus, we can feel this! Life with Jesus feels as if you are truly living, not just surviving this world. The hope of heaven and the richness of walking with Jesus helps us to endure this life and to have joy in it! Praying your day is life-giving as you walk with Jesus!

Journal WHAT GOD SPOKE TO ME · MY PRAYER REQUESTS

_____

_____

_____

_____

_____

_____

_____

_____

_____

_____

_____

_____

_____

"*Death is swallowed up in victory. O death, where is your victory? O death, where is your sting?*"

~ 1 CORINTHIANS 15:54b-55 (NKJV) ~

Our verses today seem as though they should be shouted in a stadium by millions, proclaiming Christ's triumphant victory over death! Jesus paid it all, and we get to reap the bountiful blessings: death without sting, eternal life! We are imperishable and our souls, our very essence, will be with Jesus forever. What a priceless gift we have been given, friends. On this Good Friday, as we stop to remember what Jesus did for us, remember to look back with a heart of gratefulness, and forward with a heart of hope!

We hope these past 30 days have been an encouragement to your heart, mind, and soul! God's word is so incredibly GOOD and powerful. We pray that this challenge has drawn you closer to the Lord and helped form a habit in your life to spend sweet time with Jesus every day!

Journal ~ WHAT GOD SPOKE TO ME · MY PRAYER REQUESTS

_____

_____

_____

_____

_____

_____

_____

_____

_____

_____

_____

_____

_____

_____

_____

Come to the Garden

Love Your Children

~ Week One ~

"But seek first his kingdom and His righteousness, and all these things will be given to you as well."
~ Matthew 6:33

Dear Mama,

Do you know that God chose you to be the mother of your children? He will give you the strength to raise them too! With Him, you have what it takes! Ask the Holy Spirit to help you today and every day.

The Bible tells us in James 1:5 (NIRV),"If any of you needs wisdom, you should ask God for it. He will give it to you. God gives freely to everyone and doesn't find fault."

God will also give you the wisdom you need to raise your children. He will fill you with His unconditional love for them. He will give you the joy in the journey if you seek Him first! "But seek first his kingdom and his righteousness, and all these things will be given to you as well" (Matthew 6:33).

Hug your children first thing in the morning. Remind that you *love* them, that you are *glad* God gave them to you, and that He has *great* plans for their lives!

Mama, you can do *all* things through Christ (Philippians 4:13 NKJV)! He is here to help you raise great men and women of God.

Thankful for you,
Kathryn Egly and the Help Club For Moms Team

> **"** *If you want to change the world,*
> *go home and love your family.* **"**
> ~ Mother Theresa

Intro ~ Love Your Children

Mom Tips

By: Leslie Leonard

"Her children rise up and call her blessed; her husband also, and he praises her." ~ Proverbs 31:28 (NKJV)

The Wise Woman Builds Her Spirit

- Read Galatians 5:22-23. Take note of the different fruits of the Spirit. Write them on your 3x5 cards or on your bathroom mirror. Take a moment every morning while you are getting ready to ask yourself if you are a walking example of each fruit. Pray for wisdom in the areas where you struggle.

The Wise Woman Loves Her Husband

- Clean out your husband's vehicle. Take time to clean the windows and wipe down the seats and cup holders. He will appreciate the gesture and the time spent.

- Slip a note in your husband's bag this week. Thank him for all his hard work and time spent away from home. If your husband does not carry a bag, be creative: send him an email or tuck it in his lunch.

The Wise Woman Loves Her Children

- Choose your favorite cookie recipe and make some cookies with your little people. Let them help measure, stir, and get the cookies ready to bake. Sure, it's going to be a little messy, but the smiles (and cookies) are a great reward.

- Before you speak out in correction to your children this week, bend down to their level and put your arm around them. Tell them you love them and what you would like to see them do in the future. You will be surprised at how well they respond.

The Wise Woman Cares For Her Home

- Spend 15 minutes two days this week organizing a specific area of your home that needs attention. Set a timer and stop when it goes off.

- Know what is for dinner by 9:00 a.m. three days this week. Remember to defrost any meat, etc.

These commandments that I give you today are to be on your hearts.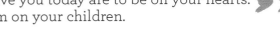
Impress them on your children.
~ Deuteronomy 6:6-7

"The cost of discipleship is high, but the cost of non-discipleship is even higher."
~ David Platt

- Call your prayer partner for your 10-minute prayer call. If you are having continual difficulty connecting with your prayer partner, pray and ask God for wisdom about what to do. If you feel that she is no longer interested in praying together call her and ask her about it. She may have a good reason for being unable to pray. Always assume the best! If she says that she can't be your prayer partner right now, pray and ask God to bring you someone else. Be on the lookout for this new prayer partner. God will bring her to you!

- Pray that God will reveal His desires for your family as you seek Him this morning.

- Read Deuteronomy 6:1-9, and write verses 4-7 in your journal.

Daily Discipleship for Children

By: Tara Davis

There are a multitude of voices in today's society beckoning us as mothers, each with their own passion and fervor. They preach the "best ways" to feed, parent, discipline, and educate our children. If we are not careful, we can easily find ourselves drowning in guilt over our decisions and differences. But there is one voice, filled with freedom and ringing clear above the rest—it is the voice of the Lord—and His is the only one that truly matters (Galatians 1:10).

Dear sister, God's commandment to us as mothers is very clear. We are to teach our children about the Lord, to involve Him in every aspect of our day, and to train our children in His ways. What a privilege we are given! As parents, we are the only people in the lives of our children charged with directing them on the path of righteousness! Therefore, if we do not feed them on the Word of God, who will?

We are called to raise children who are worshipers of God, who grow up to be satisfied in His love, and who are awestruck by the King of the universe! Considering our current culture, it is important that our children know who they are in the light of Jesus. When the world entices them, our children must recognize that their identity and value is found in Christ alone (1 Peter 2:9).

To disciple our children in the Word and ways of the Lord, it is imperative that we ourselves follow Him daily! When we shine the light of Jesus, worship Him with our whole heart, and share His tender mercy and grace, we take the first steps in making disciples of our children!

God is equipping you to bring Christ into your family life. His yoke is easy and his burden is light. He will give you the wisdom and desire you need to direct your children!

As a starting point in creating a family culture focused on discipleship, below are a few ideas to help you direct your children daily to the feet of Jesus. We are praying for you as you seek the Lord and point your children to Him!

1. **Worship Together Through His Word**
   - Choose a time of day to consistently practice family worship. Include your husband or make it a special time with just you and your children. Read God's Word or a children's devotional, and discuss as deeply as time and your children's maturity allow.
   - In addition to your own Bible, here are some of our favorite resources:
     - *Jesus Storybook Bible* by Sally Lloyd-Jones
     - *Action Bible* by Doug Mauss
     - *Leading Little Ones to God* by Marian M. Schoolland

2. **Memorize Scripture**
   - There are many free online resources offering Bible verse memorization plans for children young and old. Older children may also enjoy the Fighter Verse app for jumping into Scripture memory.
   - God's Word is like honey on our lips (Psalm 119:103). Keep something sweet on hand as a treat when practicing weekly Bible verses. Children will form a positive association with studying God's Word and hiding it in their hearts.
   - Scripture is a treasure to our souls. Reward children for verses memorized by keeping a "treasure box" filled with little gifts.

3. **Sing Praises**
   - Make a joyful noise to the Lord (Psalm 98:4)! Sing praise songs to Jesus. Your children do not care whether or not you have a beautiful voice, and neither does the Lord!
   - Play worship music throughout the day to keep hearts focused on the Lord.
   - Check out *Songs for Saplings* or *Seeds Family Worship*. These songs are a fantastic way to deliver Scripture to children.
   - Choose a meaningful hymn for your child that they can cling to through times of joy and trial. Additionally, for a fantastic children's hymn study, check out *Hymns for a Child's Heart* by Joni Erickson Tada.

4. **Pray With and Over Your Children**
   - Make a prayer jar filled with the names of people and topics to pray over. Choose a couple each day and pray together.
   - Download a prayer calendar on The Voice of the Martyrs website to guide you in praying for those around the world who need Jesus.
   - Pray over your children in the quiet of the night after they are asleep. Pray that they will have a heart to know God (Jeremiah 24:7), that they will be salt and light for Jesus (Matthew 5:13-16), and that they will know and show the love of their Father (1 John 4:19). There are many Scriptures to pray over your children!
   - Quickly pray out loud with your children when they feel frustrated, sad, hurt, or sick. Thank God together for daily joys.

5. **Bring God into Every Aspect of the Day**
   - Notice God's gifts with your children. The chirping birds, the cool breeze, the flickering flame of a candle—all are God's love gifts to us. Take it a step further by keeping a family journal to track God's little blessings.
   - Encourage your children to be the hands and feet of Jesus. How can they show the love of Christ to people within your home and lives? Let them brainstorm, and help them put one plan into action each week.
   - Share with your children what God is teaching you. They will replicate the relationship they witness you pursuing with Him.

Questions to Ponder
- Which of these ideas resonate with you? Will you commit to bringing the Lord into your child's daily life?

Faith-Filled Ideas
Start small. Pick a couple of ideas, and work toward daily consistency. Soon you will have developed a habit that will instill the gospel and an amazing love for Jesus in your children's hearts. These habits will follow your children throughout their lives. However, this list is not a formula for success. You must seek the Lord to find what will work for your own unique, beautiful family.

journal

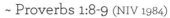
"Listen, my son, to your father's instruction and do not forsake your mother's teaching. They will be a garland to grace your head and a chain to adorn your neck.
~ Proverbs 1:8-9 (NIV 1984)

"Tell me and I forget, teach me and I may remember, involve me and I will learn."
~ Benjamin Franklin

- It is time to submit to the Lord and listen to His voice. Start your day with Him if you can, and let Him rouse your spirit awake. Even if you are still sleepy, it is amazing how time in His Word and in prayer can give a tired mama the energy she needs!

- Read Proverbs 1:8-9 and write the verses in your journal. Realize that God wants two beautiful things to happen—for us to instruct and teach our children, and for our children to accept these instructions from us. Spend a few moments praying about these verses.

Giving our Children more Responsibilities in Love

By: Rachel Jones

We recently had a fourth baby, and with his arrival, I have had to lean on my three daughters to take responsibility for things I had previously done myself. Can I admit something? This has been hard for me! I have the tendency to be the type of mother who would rather do the household chore or job myself because it is easier. Involving my kids can often be messy, annoying, and actually cause the chore to take longer. Do you agree with me, mamas?! However, I know this way of thinking and approaching responsibilities is wrong. We need to allow our children to learn by our instruction. Even though they will mess up in the beginning, teaching them is what we are called to do, and we are equipping them to be more capable human beings in the process.

Ephesians 6:4 says, regarding our children, we are to "bring them up in the training and instruction of the Lord." We should not be relying on their friends, our neighbors, or even television shows to model how to do household jobs and more importantly, how to take responsibility for their actions and messes. The Lord has spoken to me time and time again about this, and in writing this Bible study, my prayer is that I can change my ways and encourage you, mamas, to do the same. As mothers, we need to take the time to show our children how to do the dishes, fold their laundry, and empty the trash. We need to consistently allow them to mess up and still praise their efforts, even if they are doing the job in a less than perfect way.

Another important aspect of teaching your children more responsibilities is teaching them to have good attitudes. While completing jobs around the house yourself, I want to challenge you to do them with a joyful and grateful heart. Ultimately, our children strive to be like us, and they are always watching with their curious eyes. Don't we want them to see a mama who is thankful she has floors to clean and trash to collect? Children will do their chores begrudgingly: let's endeavor to show them not only how to complete a job, but that it can be done in good spirits as well!

After all, we eventually want our children to accept ownership for a task or chore and to do it without being told. Our prayer is that our children will do the job because it needs to be done and accept that it is their obligation to do it. This is called teaching our children responsibility! We need to model Proverbs 22:6 (NKJV) and, "train up a child in the way he should go..." This is the will of God for us as parents! In this process, we have to give up control of the jobs being done exactly as we would like them to be done. By allowing our children to "do it their way," we are championing a feeling of pride, accomplishment, and joy in their little hearts.

In the end, accountability, responsibility, and obedience, are what the Lord demands of our children, and we have the honor to model and teach them these qualities. We will be doing our children a huge disservice if we don't rise to this vital occasion. Over time, I have observed a beautiful principle—the children most accountable to act responsibly are the happiest and most secure in love and grounded in good will—in His good will.

Questions to Ponder

- How are you doing in this area of mothering? Write down a few ways you could do a better job in your journal. How can you give up control in your home?

- Are your kids doing regular chores around the house? And are they doing those jobs with a cheerful heart? Below is a helpful list of realistic jobs for your children. Try implementing a couple of them in your home this month.

Faith-Filled Ideas

Ok mamas! I am so honored to encourage and nudge you in the right direction towards training your children. I have compiled a list of simple jobs for different age groups. Use it! Accept this challenge and change the way your household is run.

3-5 years old

1. Empty the plastic cups, bowls, and plates from the dishwasher
2. Wipe down the front of the fridge, oven, and doors with a wet washcloth
3. Put away toys and straighten books on the bookshelf
4. Clean off the kitchen table
5. Fold towels and washcloths
6. Make their beds

6-8 years old

1. Fold all of their own laundry and put away in closet/dresser
2. Gather all of the trash cans from around the house and empty in a large bag
3. Empty the entire dishwasher except for the sharp knives
4. Wipe down the countertops in the kitchen and bathroom
5. Sweep floors
6. Empty the litter box if you have a cat
7. Fill your pet's food and water bowl

9-11 years old

1. Dust

2. Help with meal prep

3. Wash dishes

4. Pull weeds and tend to the garden if you have one

5. Wash the windows/mirrors with glass cleaner

6. Vacuum

7. Clean the sinks and toilets in the bathroom

Once a child is 12 years old, he or she should be doing all of the same household chores as you and your husband. Now is the time to really begin teaching and training your children to live on their own one day. Remember, as always, you do YOU, and we are praying for you!

Journal

_____
_____
_____
_____
_____
_____
_____
_____
_____
_____
_____
_____
_____
_____
_____
_____
_____

> **"** Be very careful, then, how you live—
> not as unwise but as wise, making the most of every opportunity. **"**
>
> ~ Ephesians 5:15-16a

"We must use time wisely and forever realize that the time is always ripe to do right."
~ Nelson Mandela

- It's time to meet with your Father! I pray He will help you make the most of the time you spend today. Quiet your mind, relax your body, and listen to what the Spirit is whispering to you.

- Read Ephesians 5:15-17 in both the NIV (above), ESV, and NKJV. Write one version in your journal. Reading multiple versions of the same passage provides a deeper understanding of scripture.

Redeeming Time

By: Heather Doolittle

One evening, I was sitting on the couch after a long day. It had started out well. My husband was on a business trip, so I planned a nice evening with my girls. Then bedtime came, and chaos broke out— hitting, yelling, and arguing, all out of nowhere. I was totally blindsided! How could we transition from a nice evening together to hair-pulling and yelling so quickly?!

I responded calmly...at first. Then came the talking back and yelling at *me*—the thoughtful mom who had spent the last two hours catering to everyone else's delights. I soon found myself shouting, and I could hear the Holy Spirit speaking to me in the midst of the chaos. As I pointed out to my children that their behavior was bringing our girls' night to a terrible end, the Spirit showed me how my harsh tone was undoing my careful efforts to pour love into my children's hearts.

After the night's battle ended and the children went to bed, I sat alone in silence. Then God reminded me of a sermon I heard years ago. The pastor encouraged parents to feed into their children's hearts and lives as much as possible while they're young because parents lose much of their influence by the time their children are around the age of 12. My heart sank at the realization that my oldest daughter—the one yelling—had recently turned 12. I pondered her subtle but swift transformations: updating her childish style, sleeping later, sitting on the couch next to me instead of on top of me, and spending more time entertaining herself.

All of these changes appear to be progress—in fact, they might be answers to prayers I made ten years ago! I am glad to see my daughter becoming (generally) more civilized as she ages; however, it is obvious that my time with her is fleeting. She is maturing into a woman, and my Father reminded me how important it is to pull her close and make the extra effort to reach her heart while I still can.

This evening helped me to better understand Psalm 90:12, "Teach us to number our days, that we may gain a heart of wisdom." How does numbering my days produce a wise heart? I've always applied this verse to my total number of days on earth—my life's end—but there is so much more to it. Every season, every phase, every day is a precious gift from our Father. Soaking in this truth not only cultivates gratitude and joy, but also wisdom. By numbering my days, I can live wisely, making the most of every opportunity to model a godly life and disciple my children and loved ones.

I was ashamed of the way I had acted that night, not at all resembling Jesus in my temperament. As my heart softened toward my children, I forgave them completely and realized I needed to model Jesus to them through humility and repentance. After reflection and prayer, I went to each of my children and apologized for my outburst. I didn't make excuses or condemn their behavior leading up to my yelling. I explained that God showed me that my behavior was wrong, and I would try to respond better next time. Even more importantly, I demonstrated that I love them enough to forgive them even before they apologize or repent.

The New King James Version of Ephesians 5:16 says to redeem the time. The definition of redeem is "to make amends for, to offset." This charge to redeem our time is certainly not something we can do on our own. We cannot offset time, and we can only make amends by investing further time. However, God is not bound by time; He can work in the past. He can take the precious moments we've squandered, whether it is hours or years, and He can redeem it for His purpose. We cannot relive the past, but God can put our imperfect pasts to good use. He will show us how to salvage our sin and mistakes for His purpose and glory. All we need to do is ask and obey.

Questions to Ponder

- Think about this past week. What activities or thoughts wasted your time? What can you do differently going forward?

- Do you have a bad habit that is consistently draining your time and energy? For me, it usually involves using media to tune out of life: checking Facebook, surfing Pinterest, or shopping online. Pray about how to sacrifice this area to God. If media is your issue, disconnect your WiFi during quiet time or before bed (don't forget to turn off cellular data on your phone too).

- Do you feel guilty over wasted time or missed opportunities? There is no condemnation for this is Christ Jesus (Romans 8:1)! Ask for forgiveness, and move on, committing to improve and realizing you'll inevitably stumble and need forgiveness again.

Faith-Filled Ideas

Whether it is by wasting time, harboring bitterness, or losing our tempers, we all sin and fall short of God's purpose (Romans 3:23). However, there is hope. We can take all our sins and cares to our Father every day, and He will consistently forgive us and cover over our iniquity. God's mercies are new every morning (Lamentations 3:23).

Not only do I ask God to forgive my sins every night, but I also ask Him to right my wrongs. Sometimes I must atone for my sins by apologizing, but other times there is simply nothing I can do to make amends. Instead of wallowing in guilt over my failure, I pray Scripture over it. God has given us great promises. Claim those promises and surrender your will to Him!

Here are some of the Scriptures I pray to cover over my sins when...

- **I feel as though I've failed my children:**

   "All your children will be taught by the Lord, and great will be their peace" (Isaiah 54:13).

- **I am faced with a tough decision:**

   "If any of you lacks wisdom, you should ask God, who gives generously to all without finding fault, and it will be given to you" (James 1:5).

- **I don't have faith:**

  "I do believe; help me overcome my unbelief!" (Mark 9:24).

  "Those who know your name will trust in you, for you, Lord, have never forsaken those who seek you" (Psalm 9:10).

- **I feel attacked on all fronts:**

  "Submit yourselves, then, to God. Resist the devil, and He will flee from you. Come near to God, and He will come near to you" (James 4:7-8a).

- **I am in the midst of a difficult season:**

  "For our light and momentary troubles are achieving for us a eternal glory that far outweighs them all" (2 Corinthians 4:17).

- **I need God to change my heart:**

  "Be completely humble and gentle; be patient, bearing with one another in love" (Ephesians 4:2).

journal

_____

_____

_____

_____

_____

_____

_____

_____

_____

_____

_____

_____

_____

_____

_____

_____

_____

Love Your Children

Food for the Soul

"It is written, 'Man shall not live by bread alone, but by every word that proceeds from the mouth of God,'" ~ Matthew 4:4

Several years ago, I learned the importance of listening to and obeying God. During that time, I felt the Lord tell me that our family needed to slow down and spend more quality time together. We were so busy and constantly going from place to place in a busy blur. I felt my children needed more simple family time.

Thus, the family night was born. Now, every Friday night, we snuggle up together on the couch for a family movie or we play a game. We often start with homemade pizza, and our kids love it. We gather around the table with all of our favorite toppings and have fun building pizzas together. As an added bonus, they get to make their own personal pizzas!

By listening to Christ and instituting a weekly family night, we have changed our family patterns. We have become closer to one another and closer to Christ. This was our intentional way to show our children love—by spending quality time together.

When you take the time to listen to the Lord, He will speak to you. Romans 8:14 says, "For those who are led by the Spirit of God are the children of God." When you obey what He tells you, He will bless you immensely! Being intentional about slowing our family down and taking the time to spend quality time with our children fills their love buckets, which in turn has blessed my husband and me as well. It has created memories for our kids that I hope they will always hold dear and cherish.

HOMEMADE PIZZA DOUGH   By: Brandi Carson

Ingredients:

1 package (or 2 ½ tsp.) of active dry yeast

1 tsp. honey

1 cup warm water (no more than 115 degrees or it will kill the yeast)

3 cups bread flour (or all-purpose)

1 tsp. kosher salt

1 tbsp. extra virgin olive oil.

Directions:

1. In a small bowl, dissolve honey and yeast in the warm water.

2. In a stand mixer, or large bowl, combine flour and salt. Mix with a dough hook attachment until well combined.

3. On low speed, combine yeast mixture and oil with the flour mixture. Continue mixing with dough hook on low speed until mixture comes cleanly away from bowl. May take up to five minutes.

4. Turn dough out onto a clean surface and knead by hand for a few minutes longer or until the dough is firm and smooth.

5. Oil a large bowl and place the dough in the bowl. Flip the dough so it is well coated with oil. Cover with plastic wrap and let rise for 30-45 minutes, or until doubled in size.

6. Preheat your oven to 450 degrees.

7. Now your dough is ready to make into a pizza. You can either cut it into half for smaller pizzas or make one large pizza.

8. Dust your work surface lightly with flour, and either roll your dough out or spread it out with your fingers.

9. Now add whatever sauce and toppings your family likes. Top with cheese.

10. Bake anywhere from 12-18 minutes depending on the thickness of your crust and the size of your pizza.

Love Your Children

~ Week Two ~

*"If any of you lacks wisdom, you should ask God,
who gives generously to all without finding fault,
and it will be given to you."*

~ James 1:5

Dear Sister,

Mothers love their children. There is no question about that. We would lay down our lives to save our children. We will sacrifice so that they do not have to go without, and the thought of losing them strikes fear to our very core. We love them, oh yes, we love them, but do we love them well? That does not come as easily. Loving our children well takes discipline, forethought, and intentionality. Loving them well takes the power of the Holy Spirit.

I am so thankful for the way the Help Club for Moms team is always pointing us to Jesus. They say over and over, "Pray and ask God...pray and ask God." He knows your situation. He has all the answers. James 1:5 says, "If any of you lacks wisdom, you should ask God, who gives generously to all without finding fault, and it will be given to you."

Each of our stories, our puzzles, is different. No two are alike. Chances are what works for one mom may not work for another. And that is why we need to pray and ask God for wisdom in our situations. We need Him to lead us and guide us in the way we should go. Isaiah 40:11b says, "He gently leads those that have young."

I pray that as you read these studies, you will cling to that promise. I pray you will hear the voice of the Lord and that He will show you ways you can intentionally love your children well. With God all things are possible!

Love and blessings,
Jennifer Valdois and the Help Club For Moms Team

> ❝ *Life is relationships; the rest is just details.* ❞
> ~ *Gary Smalley*

Mom Tips

By: Leslie Leonard

"Her children rise up and call her blessed; her husband also, and he praises her." ~ Proverbs 31:28 (NKJV)

The Wise Woman Builds Her Spirit

- Keep working on your prayer binder for 2 days this week, but keep it short (only 15-20 minutes). Remember you can easily put your prayers on your phone too.
- Listen to a Help Club for Moms video from our Facebook page while you are folding laundry or matching socks this week.

The Wise Woman Loves Her Husband

- Forego a favorite treat (like a latte) and save the money for a special night out or a gift for your husband. Maybe he has mentioned wanting something in passing for which you can save up and surprise him by practicing some self-control.
- Give your husband 15 minutes after he gets home from work to decompress. Greet him, then let him be for a few minutes. Allow him some time to let the work day go. He will be a better partner if he is not pushed right into the thick of things for the evening.

The Wise Woman Loves Her Children

- Pick a childhood favorite chapter book to read at bedtime. You will enjoy reading it to your children, and the joy of reading is contagious. You will all find yourselves looking forward to bedtime this week!
- Take a minute during your quiet time to write a note of encouragement to each of your children. Tuck the notes under their pillows for them to find when they go to bed or drop them in the mail if your children are grown. Be sure to remind them that they are eternally loved by Jesus.

The Wise Woman Cares For Her Home

- Get in the habit of making a "6 Most Important" list before you go to bed. Simply pray about what the most important things are that God wants you to get done the next day and write down the top six. Cross them off during the day as you accomplish them.
- Do the "5 o'clock pick-up" for four days this week. Put on some favorite music, set a timer for 15 minutes, and you and your children go through the main living areas and pick up everything, everywhere. Give each of your children a basket in which to put their things and then have them put away their found items. Stop after 15 minutes.

Let everyone who is thirsty come. Let anyone
who wishes to take the water of life as a gift.
~ Revelation 22:17b (NRSV)

"When we come to Him (Jesus) with an empty cup, He will fill it, often beyond our capacity to receive. He is truly living water, a manifestation of the love of God."
~ M. Heaps

- It's time to call your prayer partner! Make it quick if you must, but having a friend to pray with you and for you is one of life's greatest blessings.

- Dear mom, come to Jesus and get refreshed today! His deep well of living water never runs dry.

- Read John 4:5-42. As you study and meditate, remember you are not wanting mere knowledge about God: His Word is a personal gift so you can know Him. He desires intimacy, to fill you until you are overflowing with His Spirit.

Jesus — Our Living Water

By: Mari Jo Mast

I feel challenged as I read this beautiful story of the woman at the well. Jesus saw beyond his own physical thirst and recognized her spiritual hunger. She was a Samaritan; He was a Jew. Everyone knew Jews didn't communicate or talk with unclean pagans in those days. He knew her background—her deepest, ugliest secrets—yet still He loved her and took the time to interact with her. He spoke life-giving words that gave hope to pull her out of her sin.

As a Mom this moves me: Unlike Jesus and the woman at the well, my children are my own flesh and blood. It's so easy to be selfish. Can I look beyond my own physical wants to see their true hunger? Though I see them at their very worst, can I look deeper into their souls and ignite their true potential by speaking the words of Jesus instead of my own? Do I see their God-given potential through Him?

I've learned from experience: Correcting our kids with our own dim vision can never, ever permanently fix them. Our own pat answers cannot remedy a sin problem. Our love must go much deeper.

My heart cries out to the Father to be filled with all the fullness of Christ. I want His life to empower, to help connect the dots, to fill the God-shaped deficit in my children's hearts with life from the heart of the Father, to feed them Truth and to show them the Way.

Jesus said in Matthew 11:28-30 (NASB), "Come to Me, all who are weary and heavy-laden, and I will give you rest. Take My yoke upon you and learn from Me, for I am gentle and humble in heart, and you will find rest for your souls. For My yoke is easy and My burden is light."

Sweet mama, how easy it is to forget we have nothing to offer in our own strength and natural abilities. Empty or stale cisterns cannot feed our children.

We need a living, vital relationship with Jesus. He is our answer. Together let's go to the River. Let's drink deep—lean heavily on the Spirit who helps us in our weakness. Let's lead our children to the water He offers today. Fresh, clean, and satisfying, it never runs dry!

Questions to Ponder

• Can I see the trials in my children as an opportunity to peer into their souls?

• Can I give them what they really thirst for—Jesus?

• Will I offer a cup of cold water in His name to help them develop a craving only He can satisfy?

Faith-Filled Ideas

When you face conflict with your children throughout the day, stop and ask the Holy Spirit what you should do and say instead of reacting negatively. Be sensitive and listen. If you're not sure what to do, simply be kind.

journal

_____
_____
_____
_____
_____
_____
_____
_____
_____
_____
_____
_____
_____
_____
_____
_____
_____

This day I call the heavens and earth as witnesses against you
that I have set before you life and death, blessings and curses.
Now choose life, so that you and your children may live.

~ Deuteronomy 30:19

"Everyone needs the blessing to feel truly loved and secure about themselves."
~ John Trent, PhD author of *The Blessing*

- We believe God has *big* things in store for today's devotional as we take a look at *the Blessing* of being unconditionally loved by our Father God.

- Read Genesis 25 and 27.

- Write Deuteronomy 30:19 in your journals.

Choosing to Receive the Blessing

By: Kari Trent-Straberg and Brynne Gluch

"The healthiest homes are not the ones without problems, but the ones that love each other in the midst of those problems" - Danny Silk, *Loving on Purpose*

Simply put, *the Blessing* is a biblically-based method for families to communicate unconditional love and acceptance. Brynne and I (Kari) grew up as close friends living in homes with *the Blessing*. My family (literally) wrote the book on the subject, and Brynne's family may as well have because of their commitment to raising kids who love Jesus.

Our parents raised us with a clear message: we were loved, unique, beautiful, chosen, and full of potential. There was just one problem...We didn't believe it. As strong-minded firstborns, we both chose to forge our own paths in life despite our parents' best efforts.

For me, Kari, the choice to live life outside of Christ led to disaster. I was 24 when God physically rescued me from an extremely abusive relationship, and I surrendered my life to Him. By that account, it may seem that my childhood Blessing was ineffective. However, it was the very thing that led me home. I went to my Dad and confessed my full rebellion. As I confessed, my Dad gently stopped me and spoke a blessing that completely changed my life: "It's not about where you've been, it's about where you're going." With that Blessing, I had all the courage I needed to choose life and pursue restoration.

Like Kari, I (Brynne) spent much of my adolescence battling perfectionism while simultaneously choosing to live outside the safety of God's will. At my lowest point, I had a similar conversation with my dad in which he sat me down, prayed Philippians 4:6 over me, and said, "I promise there is still hope, freedom is waiting for you!" His belief in me in my darkest moment provided the strength I needed to choose repentance. He was right, of course, and my life transformed through surrendering to the healing power of Jesus' love.

What we'd love to communicate through our stories is that we can trust God with our kids. Scripture shows us that God is not surprised, disappointed, or afraid of failure; and there is nothing God cannot restore. And His Spirit is within us, which means our lives hold the potential to display the Father's goodness regardless of our own pasts.

Even if we do everything right, we can't control our children's responses to God. Like us, they have a choice. But by blessing our kids, we are also releasing them into the will of their heavenly Father. So we must bless and encourage ourselves with the grace to trust Him with their lives. By resolving to parent without fear, we are creating a safe environment for our kids to thrive!

Our verse today says to choose life. We choose life by raising children with the message that they are valuable to God and to us. From our family experiences, a parent who chooses *the Blessing* makes all the difference!

Questions to Ponder

- Ask yourself these questions, and journal your response:
    1. Did I experience *the Blessing* growing up?
    2. Who *Blessed* me, and what did they do to make me feel so valuable?
    3. Am I experiencing the unconditional love and *Blessing* of God as my Father?
    4. Are the people in my life experiencing my unconditional love and *Blessing*?

- If you did not receive *the Blessing* growing up, it might be hard to bestow it. Commit to spending a season allowing the Lord to heal you in these places. Call your prayer partner and ask for support as you walk through the pain of the past. Take action for yourself and your children. Freedom is waiting for you!

Faith-Filled Ideas

Try *the Blessing* with your kids! As you can see in the example below, you don't have to wait for big moments to give your child your *Blessing*. Do it daily. Make the choice to bless them, and help them *choose* their special God-given future.

BLESSING STEP	REFERENCE	EXAMPLE
Meaningful Touch	Genesis 27:26	Hold their hand, touch their shoulders, give them a hug. Every time a blessing was given in Scripture, there was the laying on of hands.
A Spoken Message	John 1:14	Pick one specific quality or character trait about them that makes them unique—be specific. Tell them out loud (write it down for them too). i.e. (*Name*), you are so compassionate.
Attaching a High Value	Genesis 27:27	Tell them how you see that one trait being displayed in them. i.e. You included your sister even when your friends didn't want to. You are a great friend to people who really need one.

BLESSING STEP	REFERENCE	EXAMPLE
Picturing a Special Future	Genesis 27:28-29	Tell them how that one trait can make a big difference in their lives, and the lives of others. i.e. Your desire to include and value others is going to change lives.
An Active Commitment	Genesis 49 Mark 10:13-16	Tell them that you are behind them 100 percent and will help them live out that trait. i.e. (*Name*), I am so proud of you. I promise that I will always be here for you and will help you continue to include others.

For more information about *the Blessing*, please refer to the book *The Blessing* by John Trent, PhD and Gary Smalley. Or visit StrongFamilies.com.

journal

_____

_____

_____

_____

_____

_____

_____

_____

_____

_____

_____

_____

_____

_____

_____

_____

Love Your Children

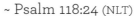 This is the day the LORD has made. We will rejoice and be glad in it.

~ Psalm 118:24 (NLT)

"Next to virtue, the fun in this world is what we can least spare."
~ Agnes Strickland

- It's time to meet with your Jesus! He is the One who loves you completely and wants you to come to Him with all of your burdens and cares. Ask Jesus to speak to your heart this week about loving your children and accepting them for who they are. Ask Him to show you your children's hearts and how to love them well in the power of the Holy Spirit.

- Read Psalm 90:12 and Psalm 113:9. Write these two powerful verses in your journal. Pray and ask the Lord to help you to enjoy your life with your family and to be aware of how short your time here on this earth really is.

Be the Fun Mom

By: Deb Weakly

Would you like an easy avenue that will lead straight to the heart of your children? Prayerfully become the *fun* mom!

Now, you might be saying, "Deb, my day in and day out life as a mom is *anything* but fun. Do you know what it's like to have mounds of laundry to do every day? There is *no* fun in that!"

Dearest mama, joy and fun are as important to your children as clean clothes to wear. These are important keys to their hearts, providing a way to give them joy-filled memories of their childhood. Your kids need to grow up in a happy home with a happy mom. Believe me, the old adage is still true: "If mama ain't happy, ain't nobody happy." Be the happy mom, and let your kids see you enjoy your life at home with them.

Here are some ideas to help:
- Pray and ask God to help you to become a fun mom, by creating a joyful, inviting, and comfortable atmosphere in your home.

- Tell you kids often how much you enjoy being their mama.

- Smile at your family—often!

- When you send them off to school or an activity, be sure to give them a warm hug and an encouraging word such as "Go M.A.D.!" which means to **Go-Make-A-D**ifference. We did this all the time with our kids and it was a good reminder to them that, even as kids, they can make a difference in their world for Jesus.

- Now is not the time for "house beautiful!" Make your home work for you! Organize it in such a way that it's easy to clean. Have cubbies for toys and games. Go to garage sales and buy games that your kids and their friends will love to play. We had a place in the kitchen where we stored our art supplies, bins of Legos, games and other fun toys.

- Be the fun mom for your kids' friends too. Make your house the fun house! Be generous with your kids' friends. Let them eat your food! Share!

- If you have teens, get a few fun and wholesome video games. I know, can you believe I suggested that? We wanted to have the house where our kids and their friends hung out, so we purchased a few fun video games for them. We popped lots of popcorn, provided a reasonable amount of candy and chips, and the kids were at our house all the time! It would be nice to think that your kids and their friends naturally want to come over, but the truth is that kids generally go to where they are welcome and where there is food and fun. Video games can be a tool, when used carefully and in moderation. Set a timer and establish limits right off the bat. Your kids need to learn self-government anyway. They won't always be in your home, and they need to learn to how to manage themselves and temper their habits.

Questions to Ponder

- In what ways can I be more fun for my kids?

- What's holding me back?

- What changes do I need to make to enjoy my life, no matter my circumstances?

Faith-Filled Ideas

Institute a *fun* new tradition in your home:

Host "Rude Fridays!" Every Friday night, when our kids were growing up, we ordered pizza, invited a couple of their friends over, and settled in for a fun evening. Our whole family would chew with our mouths open, burp, talk with our mouths full, and keep our elbows on the table. The understanding was that they had to be polite and use good table manners the other days of the week, but when Friday came around, it was all-out loud, impolite fun!! Our kids still remember those nights and how much fun they were!

Pray and ask God to help you to be a fun mom:

As my children were growing up, I kept all of my prayers in a binder. This binder has become invaluable to me over the years! I prayed these prayers many times each week. I prayed many prayers, one of which was asking God to help me to be a fun mom. Let God help you!

Here are some of my prayers:

Lord, help me to laugh more and be more fun to be around.

Lord, help me to be more winsome in the way that I talk to my family.

Help me to train my kids in a fun and non-critical way to have awesome table manners and work habits.

Jesus, show me what I can do, in the power of the Holy Spirit, to make my home more vibrant, fun, and a wonderful place to be—a place my husband, my kids, and their friends love to be!

Lord, let everyone sense your presence in our home!

Help me to play with the kids more and enjoy myself more.

Help me to laugh more and be fun to be around!

Lord, help me to be a fun mom!

journal

_____
_____
_____
_____
_____
_____
_____
_____
_____
_____
_____
_____
_____
_____
_____
_____
_____
_____
_____
_____
_____
_____
_____
_____

Love Your Children

~Beauty~
~ Week One ~

*"...They all joined together in prayer to God:
"Master and Creator of heaven, earth,
and sea and all that is in them!""*

~ Acts 4:24 (GNT)

Dear Sweet Mama,

We've all heard the cliché "stop and smell the roses," meaning to take time out of one's busy schedule to enjoy or appreciate the beauty of life. It is so important to take this often used saying to heart though and filter it through God's Word so we can truly appreciate its value.

"Ever since the creation of the world, God's invisible qualities—God's eternal power and divine nature—have been clearly seen, because they are understood through the things God has made" (Romans 1:20 CEB). In this verse, we learn that we can grasp God's divine nature by seeing what He has made and experiencing His creation! The beauty we experience in nature now has greater meaning and intention. God wants to use everything He made to draw us closer to Him and to help us understand Him better.

We've all probably felt that amazing feeling you get when you gaze out on the majesty of the land from the high peak of a mountain, or when you magnify a leaf and see a whole microscopic world open up, displaying the tiny intricacies of life. It's these examples that draw us closer to God. He is the "Master and Creator of heaven, earth, and sea, and all that is in them" (Acts 4:24b GNT).

I pray that this week, dear mama, you will have a moment to focus on the pure beauty of God's creation—whether it is on a hike or simply smelling a rose in a vase on your counter. I pray in that moment, God will draw you closer to Him and help you see through His eyes.

With love,
Kristall Willis and the Help Club For Moms Team

❝ *I love to think of nature as an unlimited broadcasting station, through which God speaks to us every hour, if we only will tune in.* **❞**
~ George Washington Carver

Mom Tips

By: Leslie Leonard

"He has made everything beautiful in its time. Also, He has put eternity in their hearts, except that no one can find out the work that God does from beginning to end." ~ Ecclesiastes 3:11 (NKJV)

The Wise Woman Builds Her Spirit

- Write on your notecards or bathroom mirror or record on your phone the following verses: Song of Solomon 4:7, Psalm 139:14, 1 Peter 3:3-4, and Romans 5:6. Pick your favorite to memorize by the end of the week.
- Journal one day this week about beauty and what it means to you. Keep Luke 6:45 in mind while journaling.

The Wise Woman Loves Her Husband

- When saying your nightly prayers this week, be sure to take a moment to thank God for your husband. Be specific about the blessings he has brought into your home and life. Ask God to strengthen your relationship and bring you closer together.
- Make your husband a special meal or dessert this week. Choose something that he loves but you do not make very often.

The Wise Woman Loves Her Children

- Journal about each of your children's attributes this week. Write down all the wonderful strengths and passions you see in them. Ask God for wisdom on how to guide them to grow in these areas.
- Grab your art supplies and have your children create some beauty for your home this week. Proudly display their artwork in a shared area of your home. Share the artwork with an elderly neighbor or drop it in the mail to the grandparents!

The Wise Woman Cares For Her Home

- Create a new centerpiece for your dining room table this week. Purchase some inexpensive flowers from the market or pull out that vase or decorative bowl you keep in the cupboard.
- Clear any clutter or paperwork from your kitchen this week. Shred, throw away, or file anything that does not belong. Put items away that are in the wrong area of your home. Commit to not letting paperwork pile up again.

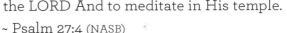

> One thing I have asked from the LORD, that I shall seek:
> That I may dwell in the house of the LORD all the days of my life,
> to behold the beauty of the LORD And to meditate in His temple.
>
> ~ Psalm 27:4 (NASB)

"Look for beauty where it is not supposed to be found."
~ Claes Oldenburg, sculptor

- Call your prayer partner for your 10-minute prayer call. Keep trying to connect until you get to pray together. This tiny habit of praying regularly with a friend will truly change your life! It has changed mine!

- Sweet friends, take a moment to soak in God's beauty and goodness around you. So often, I let whatever is stealing my attention overshadow the amazing gifts God has given me: a husband who is there through the good and the bad, children who love and forgive with ease, and friends who encourage me to live well. I pray that you will see the beauty in your surroundings and relationships, forgetting all your cares as you meet with God today.

- Read Psalm 27:4 and write it in your journal.

Unexpected Beauty

By: Heather Doolittle

Last winter, my grandfather passed away. He was a strong, godly man who worked and prayed for everyone around him until the day he died. I hadn't seen him much over the past few years—the distance proving prohibitive as his health declined and my family grew. However, despite my sadness in his passing, I felt a deep peace knowing he had led a full, godly life. I imagine God greeted him in heaven with the words, "Well done, good and faithful servant." As we gathered photos of my grandpa's life, letters from his loved ones, and meaningful songs for the memorial, the pain of death and separation was eclipsed by the beauty and joy he left behind.

I felt God near as I listened to Kristen DiMarco's "It is Well with my Soul" at the memorial and began to comprehend the beauty in my grandfather's transition from this life into the next. He experienced sin and pain as everyone does, but God's love is so great that it overshadows all else. I witnessed how God used an imperfect but faithful man to bring a bit of His eternal glory to this Earth. Through Jesus' healing power, God covered over all our sins and struggles with His beautiful, glorious love.

It's easy to recognize God's love and beauty in the joys of life, but what about in the midst of pain and struggles? These situations magnify God's glory and beauty all the more if we keep our focus on Him and remain steadfast in faith. This year, I have challenged myself to seek beauty in all aspects of life—especially in that which is mundane or painful. In looking for beauty and goodness, I have found it in unexpected places. You see, God's goodness fills the Earth; it is easy to find when you're looking for it.

Beauty

The heavens declare the glory of God; the skies proclaim the work of His hands. (Psalm 19:1)

Embracing beauty is a form of living with gratitude, a constant awareness that God is the provider of everything good. **Our heavenly Father is the architect of beauty; it is the fingerprint He leaves on everything He touches.** The key to seeing beauty in all situations is finding God in them. God has inserted beauty and goodness into everything He has made, and so it exists wherever God is—even in earthly death. Sometimes the underlying beauty isn't apparent, but we must trust that God has a greater purpose that we do not see. Jesus told the disciples, "You don't understand now what I am doing, but someday you will" (John 13:7 NLT). Friends, I urge you to seek out the good in all situations and trust that God has a plan to redeem everything that seems bad.

I love the prophet Micah's attitude of faith when he wrote: "But me, I'm not giving up. I'm sticking around to see what God will do. I'm waiting for God to make things right" (Micah 7:7a MSG). We must have this same stance. We have a powerful Father who can make everything good and right in its own time.

Questions to Ponder

- Are there any areas of your life, your marriage, or your family in which you fail to recognize God's beautiful plan? Write them down and pray that God will help you with this. As He reveals His answer to you, write it in your journal.

- Do Micah's words touch your heart? Is there a hard situation that you're waiting on God to fix? Tell God about it, pray that He will give you wisdom about His purpose in this struggle, and say a prayer to remind yourself that He will make everything right. For God's children, all things work together for good (Romans 8:28).

Faith-Filled Ideas

Start a **Thankful Journal** with your family!

Buy a pretty prayer journal, blank journal, or sketchbook, and let your kids decorate it.

Set aside some time to teach your children what you learned in this study, and talk to them about looking for God's goodness and beauty all around you. Serve some special snacks to keep your kids quiet while you're teaching them (bonus: this will make your kids look forward to family Bible studies).

After you're done talking and listening to your children's input, play worship music while they decorate the Thankful Journal together. Some great songs that go well with this lesson: "Beautiful Things" by Gungor and "You're Beautiful" by Phil Wickham (I listen to them for free on YouTube).

After the journal has been decorated, give everyone a chance to add something. Allow your children to be creative. Don't shoot down an answer—just ask them how God's beauty is evident in that response. Help them come up with something, if necessary, so they will see that everything good comes back to God. Let them write in the journal themselves, or you could write what they dictate and give them a chance to sign it. When my kids were little, they loved adding their scribble "signature" to their entries. Let them draw pictures if they prefer, and help the little ones caption their drawings.

Keep this journal out in the open where you will see it and add to it often. Tell your kids that they can add to it too. It will be a sweet reminder of all of God's gifts—both big and little!

Journal

_____
_____
_____
_____
_____
_____
_____
_____
_____
_____
_____
_____
_____
_____
_____
_____
_____
_____
_____
_____
_____
_____
_____
_____
_____

Beauty

Give to the Lord the glory due His name...
worship the Lord in the beauty of holiness!

~ 1 Chronicles 16:29 (NKJV)

"If God is everything to us, why should we ever need anything else?!"
~ Francis Chan

- Good morning my friend! Today is a day to take an honest look at your heart and lay yourself before the feet of your merciful, loving Savior.

- Read 1 John 2:15-17. Also, read Psalm 51:1-12 and spend some time praying verse 10 to the Lord before you dig into today's study.

Refocusing Our Eyes on the Infinite Beauty of Our Lord

By: Tara Davis

Beauty

Take a look around you. Do you see how we are living as a society today? We are so consumed with ourselves and our physical beauty. We've been described as living in the "selfie-era," an age dipped in narcissism and coated with a perfectly curated, Instagram-ready finish. It's a sign of the times, really. In 2 Timothy 3:2, Paul tells us that in the last days, people will become "lovers of themselves," and here we are, so preoccupied with us. We worry unendingly about whether our nose is too big, our hair too frizzy, and if our pants make us look too chubby. I'm right there with you, my friend. It is so easy to allow thoughts of personal beauty to consume us. We have become lovers of self, not lovers of God.

So, where do we go from here? We must make a change. We must shift our perspectives. Glance away from the mirror, my friend, and look to the beauty of God's great, sacrificial love (1 Samuel 12:24). Those who follow Jesus will never need to know the ugliness of an eternity separated from Him. He saved us from hell, from death, and delivered us into a life of walking in communion with the One who is the most amazing, powerful, loving being to ever exist. It is pure beauty that we can even approach His throne (Hebrews 4:16) and that, because of Jesus, we get to come into the presence of the most Holy of Holies. And as if that wasn't enough, He put His Spirit inside us to guide us, to be our worth and our identity (John 16:13). Now that is *awesome beauty*, a beauty which far overshadows the latest makeup tutorial and new clothing trend (1 Samuel 16:7).

If we understood the finiteness of our lives here on earth, if we knew what a vapor this all is, we wouldn't worry so much about our physical appearances (James 4:14). Instead, we would be focused on the Lord and on sharing with others the beauty of a life lived in Him. We view self-esteem too highly, my friend. Our esteem is not in ourselves, but in Him. As believers, we have Him in us, and that is enough. This isn't about accepting ourselves for who we are, nor is it about feeling empowered as women. This is about shifting our focus completely away from ourselves and wholly onto our Savior, the Majesty over all creation (Matthew 22:37-38).

Do you want to live solely to reflect the beauty of your Father (Psalm 27:4)? He wants you to shine for Him, to mirror Him. He wants any beauty in you to be the simple reflection of the image of Jesus. Lord change us; change me. Make me more like you. I don't want to waste my life any longer, focused on things which matter nothing—things that will burn to ash in the end (1 Corinthians 3:9-15). Let our voices ring out in unison as women, "You are the beauty of our life, Lord. We want to live to glorify You alone."

Although our flesh may be crying "make me thinner, make me better, make me pleasing to those around me," when we submit to the Spirit of the living Christ in us, our soul sings "Holy, Holy, Holy. Give us purpose to magnify your beauty Lord. Less of me, more of You" (John 3:30). Don't silence that Spirit-voice with the words of the world. Turn away from your flesh, turn your heart toward the loving beauty of your Father (Romans 12:1).

Seek the Lord first above yourself and pray for God to transform your desires to reflect his own. When you get distracted with yourself, train your eyes to refocus on Him. Dig deep into His Word, form a relationship with Him through prayer, and seek the Holy Spirit.

We have to jump off this vanity-train, sisters. We have only one life to live for Jesus. We must lay ourselves and our desires for affirmation, down at the foot of the cross. Matthew 16:24-26 (BSB) says, "Then Jesus told His disciples, 'If anyone would come after Me, he must deny himself and take up his cross and follow Me. For whoever wants to save his life will lose it, but whoever loses his life for My sake will find it. What will it profit a man if he gains the whole world, yet forfeits his soul?'" Deny yourself and your flesh. When we deny ourselves and get over ourselves, we will live in freedom, filled with joy and peace.

Pray that God will give you a desire for Him—a desire to seek Him above yourself. We read in Proverbs 31:30, "Charm is deceptive, and beauty is fleeting; but a woman who fears the LORD is to be praised." This life and our physical bodies, are slowly passing away. Your beauty is sure to fade as well, but your relationship with the Lord is eternal, my friend. Invest your time, attention, and love wisely. To fall madly in love with your Savior is the greatest beauty you can ever seek.

Questions to Ponder
• Where do your affections lie? We can all grow closer to the Lord, desiring more of Him and less of us. Take a moment to be honest before the Lord today.

Faith-Filled Ideas
Make the time you spend caring for your body time spent caring for your spirit as well, refocusing your eyes on Jesus. Pray while you are getting ready in the morning or listen to an audio Bible app or a sermon while you are exercising or taking care of your home. Allow these daily necessities to be a time of growth in your relationship with the Lord! Use your life not to better yourself, but to glorify the Lord (John 17:4)!

journal

_____

_____

_____

_____

_____

_____

_____

_____

_____

_____

_____

_____

_____

_____

_____

_____

_____

_____

_____

_____

_____

_____

_____

Beauty

> " If then you have been raised with Christ, seek the things
> that are above, where Christ is, seated at the right hand of God.
> Set your mind on things that are above, not on things that are on earth.
> For you have died and your life is hidden with Christ in God.
> When Christ who is your life appears, then you also will appear with him in glory! "
>
> ~ Colossians 3:1-4 (ESV)

"Beauty awakens the soul to act."
  ~ Dante Alighieri

- Make time to spend with the Lord today! Curl up in your favorite spot and seek the Lord's presence. Pray that He will meet you where you are and open your eyes to see the truth of His Word.

- Read through Colossians 3:1-4 and Romans 8:18-25. Write down Colossians 3:2 in your journal and ask the Lord to help you set your mind on the things that are important to Him. Ask Him for an eternal perspective in your pursuit of beauty.

Finding Beauty in the Imperfect

By: Carmen Brown

We long for beauty. That is why print and online media, such as Pinterest, are so popular. We long for beauty in our homes, in nature, and in ourselves. We enjoy the beauty in art, music, and story. God is the great Creator of beauty. I believe that when we long for beauty in our lives, we are longing for Him—for the perfection we will have in Heaven where "we will be like him because we will see him as he is" (1 John 3:2b CSB).

I used to daydream of going to Italy and living in a beautiful home, riding my bike into town each day with a basket on the front filled with fresh fruit and bread from the market. In this dream, I also knew how to speak Italian fluently, of course. At times, this dream became an idol of sorts, a place I would go to "escape" from the difficulties of life. One day the Lord showed me that the longing for this "perfect and beautiful escape" was really a longing for Him. This was a great encouragement to me. It led me to meditate on Colossians 3:2 (NASB), which says to "set your mind on the things above, not on the things that are on earth."

Romans 8:20-21 (ESV) says, "creation was subjected to futility, not willingly, but because of him who subjected it, in hope that the creation itself will be set free from its bondage to corruption and obtain the freedom of the glory of the children of God." Even the beauty of nature that we enjoy has been dimmed by sin in the world. Romans 8:22 (ESV) says, "For we know that the whole creation has been groaning together in the pains of childbirth until now." We can get discouraged when our quest for beauty in our homes (or in ourselves) falls short. Instead of being discouraged, we need to be reminded that this world is not our home and that the whole creation is groaning and even we ourselves groan as we wait eagerly for the redemption of our bodies. And so, we hope for what we do not see. We wait for it with patience (Romans 8:23-25).

So, even in all of this imperfection, we can create beauty as a signpost of what is to come. Our creations should point those in our lives to the true, lasting beauty that can only be found in Christ. We should pursue beauty with our children, enjoy the beauty of the arts and nature with them, and show them how these things reflect the beauty of our Creator. As quoted above by Dante, "Beauty enables the soul to act." A focus on the beautiful in our homes and in our lives should reflect our focus on our Creator, who enables us to act, to move forward, and to embrace the imperfect.

Questions to Ponder

• How does your pursuit of beauty in your home or in yourself create discouragement at times? Can you refocus your pursuit of beauty in a way that gives you an eternal perspective and a hope?

Faith-Filled Ideas

Pick one of your favorite places of beauty, whether in the arts, nature, or a story, and share it with your children. Look for and show them how that beauty is a reflection of our great Creator and the greater beauty of the gospel in our lives.

journal

_____

_____

_____

_____

_____

_____

_____

_____

_____

_____

_____

_____

_____

_____

_____

Beauty

Food for the Soul

As we study Beauty this week, I find myself thinking about some of the godly women I have met in my life and what makes them so beautiful to me. Of course, it is because they love Jesus and live their lives for His glory, but what does that mean exactly?

These women are salt and light, a city on a hill, and an example of how I strive to live my life; an example of Jesus Christ. They are open-armed, full of love, compassionate, humble, and sincere. They show the love of Jesus wherever they go. This is what beauty is to me. I hope one day I can begin to represent this kind of biblical beauty. A great place to begin is 1 Peter 4:8-9: "Above all, love each other deeply, because love covers over a multitude of sins. Offer hospitality to one another without grumbling."

Love the people in your life whether they be longtime friends, new friends, young, or old. A great way to do that is to open your home. You could host a new mom you just met, a friend going through a difficult time, or just have a friend over to catch up. Invite them over for coffee or tea and a yummy treat. I've got an amazing recipe for scones that will make it extra special! What is more beautiful than sitting around a table with a good, hot cup of coffee (or tea) and delicious scones, having fellowship with a friend?

This is such a great recipe; you can customize it to any flavor you want! You can even make the dough ahead of time and freeze it, then bake the scones hot and fresh whenever you want! It's great for holidays and when you have guests over for breakfast.

BASIC SCONES

By: Brandi Carson

Ingredients:

2 ½ cups all-purpose flour

¼ cup sugar

1 tsp. salt

2 tsp. baking powder

½ tsp. baking soda

½ cup unsalted butter chilled and diced up into small pieces

¾ cup half and half

¼-½ cup mix-ins, like chocolate chips, raisins with cinnamon, apples, blueberries, orange zest...The possibilities are endless!

Directions:

1. In a mixing bowl, whisk together the dry ingredients.

2. Add chilled butter. Using your hands or a pastry blender, cut in the butter until the flour mixture is a crumbly coarse texture.

3. In a separate bowl, add your mix-ins and about ¼ cup of the flour mixture. Coat the mix-ins well with the flour mixture. This will help the mix-ins stick to the dough.

4. Add the coated mix-ins to the flour mixture. Stir well to combine.

5. Add the half and half and stir in gently. Stir until combined, then dump onto a floured countertop and knead until the flour is well combined. The less you mix the dough, the more tender the scones will be.

6. Being sure the countertop is still well floured, roll the dough out to about 1" to 1 ½" thickness and shaped like a rectangle or square. Cut the dough into long rows, then cut each row into individual triangles. You could also make round scones by cutting them with a biscuit cutter. Gather scraps and repeat. You can make about 20-25 small or a dozen large scones.

7. For best results chill the scones for at least half an hour or freeze them before baking. Cold butter results in tender, flaky scones. In a preheated 400 degree oven, bake large scones for 12-15 minutes or smaller scones for 8-10 minutes. Scones with fresh fruit tend to need additional baking time due to the moisture in them.

8. Dust with powdered sugar or make a simple glaze to drizzle on top. Serve.

We hope you try this recipe. It's easier than you think!

Beauty
~ Week Two ~

"You are altogether beautiful, my love;
there is no flaw in you."
~ Song of Solomon 4:7

Dear Mama,

You are beautiful. You are flawless. You are loved. You. Created and loved by the perfect God who is capable of lovingly creating nothing but perfection. *"You are altogether beautiful, my love; there is no flaw in you"* (Song of Solomon 4:7). *"And God saw everything that he had made, and behold, it was very good"* (Genesis 1:31a ESV). Such magnificent truth!

Unfortunately, this truth can be difficult to believe when we are standing in front of the full-length mirror and feel dissatisfied with the reflection, or when we consider other women around us who are either younger, thinner, curvier, taller, smaller...the list of comparisons could be endless. These judgments can cause each of us to doubt our loveliness and therefore doubt our worth.

Friend, that is the Enemy! Plain and simple. When these doubts creep into your mind and heart, replace them with truth: I am beautiful. I am flawless. I am loved and lovingly fashioned by the God who sees me as perfect in every way.

Love,
Rebekah Measmer and the Help Club for Moms Team

❝ *If you can believe the God who is perfect loves you,*
then you can believe that you are worth loving. **❞**
~ *Joyce Meyer*

Mom Tips

By: Leslie Leonard

"Charm is deceptive, and beauty is fleeting; but a woman who fears the LORD is to be praised." ~ Proverbs 31:30

The Wise Woman Builds Her Spirit

- Call your prayer partner this week. Commit to keeping your prayer time short and on topic. Write down any requests she had and pray over them for the rest of the week.

- Complete all the Help Club for Moms Bible studies this week.

The Wise Woman Loves Her Husband

- Write a note (or send a quick text) to your husband this week telling him five things you love and appreciate about him.

- Encourage your husband to read the Bible to your children this week. Choose a time that works well for everyone and where no one feels rushed. Bedtime or right after dinner are great times to pull out God's Word and read as a family.

The Wise Woman Loves Her Children

- Cook with your children this week. Have them take the lead in following the recipe and let them try to complete the task themselves. Stay close to help with any cutting or stove-top tasks. Remember to tell them how good of a job they did when you are enjoying the fruits of their labor.

- Begin your day with praise and worship music during breakfast. This is a simple way to create a calm and loving environment in the mornings. Encourage everyone to sing along while they eat their meal.

The Wise Woman Cares For Her Home

- Empty your dishwasher first thing in the morning three days this week. Now dirty dishes can go right in the dishwasher and not languish in the sink. Start the dishwasher when you head off to bed, so the dishes will be ready in the morning.

- Meal plan for the following week by Thursday. Make a detailed grocery list while you plan and check your pantry before you go shopping to avoid purchasing duplicate items. Stick to your meal plan for the entire week.

> **❝** Therefore be imitators of God, as beloved children; and
> walk in love, just as Christ also loved you and gave Himself
> up for us, an offering and a sacrifice to God as a fragrant aroma. **❞**
>
> ~ Ephesians 5:1-2 (NASB)

"Don't shine so others can see you. Shine so that through you, others can see Him."
~ C.S. Lewis

- Call your prayer partner today for your 10-minute prayer call.

- Good morning, sweet sister! God is calling you into His presence this morning. Bow your heart in surrender to Him today. He has a better plan for your life than you could ever imagine. Follow Him!

- Check out Ephesians 5:1-2 in your Bible, and write it in your journal. Look up the rest of the references as well for more in-depth study. *Always* check what you read or hear against God's Word. We are all fallible, but the Bible is your ultimate source of truth and wisdom!

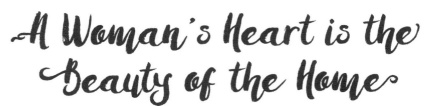

A Woman's Heart is the Beauty of the Home

By: Tara Davis

My friend, do you long to make your home a beautiful place for your family? We each have unique ways of feathering our nests. You may be a pro at decorating, have a keen organizational ability, or enjoy preparing scrumptious meals for those you love. God formed us with an innate desire to fill the world around us with beauty in some way (Ephesians 2:10). At the crux of it, we have a heart for creating a safe haven for our family, a refuge from the storms of life in which they feel comfortable, loved, and cherished.

There are a multitude of resources detailing ways to decorate, cook, or create a life-giving atmosphere in your home. However, I would challenge you to take that desire to the Giver of Life Himself. Let Him reveal His plan for your home and your heart (Proverbs 3:5-6). Despite all our best efforts, it is only when we walk in the light of Christ that our homes become the safe haven for which we are longing.

It is not so much about the beautiful atmosphere and nourishing meals you create. Candles, food, and decor are wonderful, but it is a mother's soul, beautifully lit with the glow of the Holy Spirit, that fills a home with comfort, peace, and security (Romans 15:13). When you are walking in the Spirit, my friend, your loving words and a gentleness that can only come from Jesus will fill the corners of your home and the hearts of your family. They will be drawn in by your kindness and joy, and they will be enthralled with the love of the Father as they see you walking with Him (Matthew 5:16).

Christ shining through you is what makes your home beautiful. Be the mama who looks past your aging home finishes and the smattering of toys strewn on the floor, and allow yourself to shine with the dazzling love of Jesus. This is only possible when you are absolutely captivated with the Lord yourself! Only when you want Him more than anything else in this world, when you pray that He will give you a desire for Him, and commit to spending time with Him daily, will you begin to radiate the love of Jesus to those within your walls.

Proverbs 14:1 tells us that "a wise woman builds her house." Are you building lasting, eternal qualities into your home, or is your construction only as deep as the color of your walls and the décor on your mantle? We can spend hours combing through decorating blogs. We can even build a brand new, trendy home with special, magical spaces for our children. We can light candles, turn on music, and pop homemade chocolate chip cookies into the oven, yet still have a home devoid of beauty—a home bankrupt of love, joy, and all the things God desires for our families.

His love in us is manifest in ways that bring peace and comfort to all who enter our home. He tells us that our beauty "should be...the unfading beauty of a gentle and quiet spirit, which is of great worth in God's sight" (1 Peter 3:3-4). Let the beauty of your home be found in you, my friend. Set your heart on things above as you tend to your home and all of your precious ones within (Colossians 3:1).

Now *this* is the work of motherhood, dear sister. It doesn't just happen overnight, and it is not a personality trait nor an inherent skill. Creating a safe haven home is the work of the Lord, as we walk with Him, study His Word, and let Him form us into the mothers he has created us to be (Colossians 2:6-7). Live every day for Him. Breathe in and breathe out the love of Jesus. Keep leaning into Him and His Holy Word this week, mamas! The Lord is building your house and your family through *you*!

Questions to Ponder

- Take a really good look into your heart today. Does your family see Christ in you? Does your countenance shine the light of Jesus in your home, or do your family members walk on eggshells, trying not to upset you? Pray and ask God to change you. I am praying the same thing for myself and for you, my friend!

Faith-Filled Ideas

The most soul-transforming decision you can make as a believer is spending time daily with the Lord: reading His Word, talking to Him, and meditating on His precepts throughout the day (Joshua 1:8). In this way, we should model ourselves after Moses who consistently climbed up a literal mountain to spend time with our most holy, awesome, beautiful Creator. Through their fellowship, the Lord caused Moses' face to shine, to radiate as evidence of God's glory to all he came in contact with (Exodus 34:29-35). Let that be your motivating desire, that your whole life would shine from just being with God, in His presence. "Climb up the mountain" daily to spend time with your Father, regardless of how hard or inconvenient it may be. If you do this, my friend, your home will not need candles or glitzy furnishings to provide a beautiful atmosphere, because you will be radiating the warm glow of Christ's love (2 Corinthians 3:18).

Beauty

Journal

Beauty

> How beautiful on the mountains are the feet of those who bring good news,
> who proclaim peace, who bring good tidings, who proclaim salvation,
> who say to Zion, 'Your God reigns!'
>
> ~ Isaiah 52:7

"For every minute you remain angry, you give up sixty seconds of peace of mind."
~ Ralph Waldo Emerson

- I invite you to open up your heart to God in this quiet moment and ask Him what it looks like for you to be beautiful to those in your care. What is the most beautiful way you can live that sparks life and beauty in the souls around you?

- Consider writing the following verses in your journal: Romans 8:6 & 1 Peter 3:3-4.

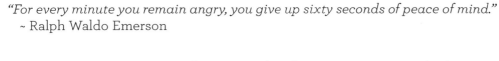

How Beautiful are the Gentle Peacemakers

By: Jennifer Kindle

Most say beauty is in the eyes of the beholder, but I dare suggest that beauty isn't only seen. I venture to say that the presence of beauty is felt; its words are heard, its heart is tasted, and its aroma intrigues the most curious of skeptics.

A wise woman who radiates grace, forgiveness, and gentleness is the most attractive woman to me. A woman who loves Jesus and abides in His presence is one who knows that true beauty is the characteristic of Christ; His likeness radiates out of the depths of her soul, which has been steeped for some time in relationship with Him.

As a mother, I've chosen to-do lists and tasks, tasks with no eternal value, over my children's hearts more times than I'd like to remember, and it's those times that I'm sure my children wouldn't perceive me as beautiful or wise at all. There's nothing wise or beautiful about me when I'm short with my children, unwilling to offer grace, or creating chaos rather than peacefully subduing it.

It's the times I've hushed the hurry and hurried the quiet that my children are the fondest of and that best represent who I want to reflect. The times when my words are apt and timely, bringing hope and restoration to a situation, are the moments my soul comes alive, and I feel the presence of the Lord is near.

The actions that we take while reflecting God's love beckon others to Him and His true beauty. The arms that hold a crying, lonely child model what beauty can be in relationships. Tender listening, more than talking, is what those around us hear the loudest. The offering of a mother's service to her family creates an appetite for what is noble and good; dying to self so others can reach their full potential is the most beautiful sacrifice of love. Random acts of kindness make the common skeptic curious. What is different about the one who just watered the beauty hidden deep in the shadow of his or her soul?

Good tidings in my home sound a lot like grace for mistakes and forgiveness for defiance. Tidings of great joy resound with the proclamation that there are second chances and new mercies every morning. When peace rules in my heart and I imprint it on my children's souls in the midst of busy chaos, the atmosphere shifts toward the greater good, and I feel the most beautiful. True beauty is found in the wise woman who responds to a negative circumstance by proclaiming with boldness that we are not forgotten and abandoned people, but cherished children of the sovereign God.

A wise woman is beautiful, not because of what is seen with physical eyes, but because of how she shifts the atmosphere when she walks into a room, carrying with her the power of her Savior. She is marked by beauty when the overflow of her heart and speech offers the grace and hope of the One who died for her.

Questions to Ponder

• Do your children feel peaceful around you, knowing you will be the first to offer grace and forgiveness?

• Do you feel beautiful by the way you parent?

Faith-Filled Ideas

Practice turning negatives into positives. Example: When they spill the milk again or break another dish, instead of letting frustration rise, ask God to help you extend grace. Offer a lending hand, assuring them that you have accidents too and that people are more important than things.

Brainstorm random acts of kindness with your children and follow through with doing them together.

Create an unhurried atmosphere in your home. Slow down and embrace the moments of your day with your children. Don't rush to the next things, but savor the smallest of moments.

Journal

> **"** For ever since the world was created, people have seen the earth and sky.
> Through everything God made, they can clearly see his invisible qualities—
> his eternal power and divine nature. So they have no excuse for not knowing God. **"**
>
> ~ Romans 1:20 (NLT)

"Never lose an opportunity of seeing anything beautiful, for beauty is God's handwriting."
~ Ralph Waldo Emerson

- I hope you have come to the Father in expectancy today! Do you have your Bible and some time? He is ready to meet with you and lead you down the path of understanding. He promises that if we seek Him, we will find Him. Refresh yourself with the story of creation found in Genesis 1.

Cultivating Hearts through God's Creation

By: Tara Fox

If beauty is God's handwriting, He penned a love letter when He created the universe. God's plan from the beginning was that we may know Him from the beauty and workings of His creation all around us.

It is valuable for us to cultivate an awareness and longing in our lives and our children's lives for nature. We are near to our Creator when we are near to His creation; to know His handiwork is to know to His heart. I want my children to become students of nature so that they clearly see God's invisible qualities. I want them to know everything there is to know about Him and to never stop learning through the power of the Holy Spirit. Developing a heart for creation in our children will produce a harvest of righteousness in their lives and the lives they touch.

Cultivate a Heart That Sees
The first step in being close to God through nature is to tune our eyes to see that "God saw all that he had made, and it was very good" (Genesis 1:31).

We have to slow down and let our eyes focus on the simple beauty that lies right outside our windows: fields of wildflowers bursting with color and variety, the stars and planets stretched vibrantly across the sky in the early morning, animals innately caring for their young, the simple goodness of household pets, trees in varying shades of green that know times long past, majestic mountain peaks that reveal our smallness, the powerful unending ocean surf, continuous ordered seasons, and the perfectly designed seed of a plant that provides bounty in season.

Cultivate a Heart That Ponders
But ask the animals, and they will teach you, or the birds in the sky, and they will tell you; or speak to the earth, and it will teach you, or let the fish in the sea inform you. (Job 12:7-9a NLT)

Beauty

Take time to watch the ant labor, the bee pollinate, the bird nest, and the spider spin. Watch the cloud rain, the wind blow, and the fire burn. We should always have this question rolling through our minds: What does this teach us about our Creator and about ourselves?

If we pay attention, God will never stop leading us to new lessons about Himself and His character. We learn and can teach our children about His provision, beauty, glory, desires, creativity, excellence, goodness, faithfulness, kindness, playfulness, and eternal nature. We can also acquire wisdom for daily living through observing natural cycles such as the hard work of sowing and reaping.

There are countless lessons to be learned from each scenario of creation. The Holy Spirit will instruct you when you have a heart that ponders.

Cultivate a Heart that Knows

> You made all the delicate, inner parts of my body and knit me together in my mother's womb. Thank you for making me so wonderfully complex! Your workmanship is marvelous—how well I know it. (Psalms 139:13-14 NLT)

Can you imagine His very hands forming you? The human body is a design marvel. Its intricacies are amazing. To study it is to become more convinced of its Creator. Each one of us must know that we are God's most magnificent creation! We must teach our children that they are made in God's image and that He absolutely delights in them. We must impart to them that they were created with a good and necessary purpose that God himself decided long ago. We will become everything God has destined for us when we know to whom we belong.

Cultivate a Heart that Cares

When we are close to nature, we develop awareness and compassion for other living things. God is for all living things, and He wants us to be also. He is tender and loving to each creature. We must be intentional to show our children how God wants us to treat His creation, specifically animals. The Bible says, "a righteous man has kind regard for the life of his animal, but even the compassion of the wicked is cruel" (Proverbs 12:10 AMP).

God has given us dominion over the animals because He is trusting us with their care. I want to teach my children to rule with kindness. How can we serve God by how we care for his creation? The Holy Spirit gives us the ability to care for everyone and everything He puts in our path. Sometimes kindness takes sacrifice on our part. Even the smallest act of compassion will not be overlooked by God.

Cultivate a Heart that Hopes

> For we know that all creation has been groaning as in the pains of childbirth right up to the present time. And we believers also groan, even though we have the Holy Spirit within us as a foretaste of future glory, for we long for our bodies to be released from sin and suffering. (Romans 8:22-23 NLT)

The groaning of creation points to God's ultimate plan of redemption. I am often grieved over the present state of creation. We see this verse spelled out each day: abortion, sickness, disease, abuse, and suffering. I long for the time when Jesus will come to make everything whole. Romans goes on to tell us that we must "wait with eager hope" (Romans 8:23 NLT).

My soul rejoices in the thought of God restoring everything to His original intention of wholeness and perfection. Let's remind our children where our hope lies. He has a plan for all of us; it's coming and it's good!

Cultivate a Heart that Praises

> From the rising of the sun to the place where it sets, the name of the LORD is to be praised. (Psalm 113:3)

Beauty ~ Week Two ~ Day Six

Beauty

Creation reminds us that we are but a speck in the universe. When we are aware of this, we are left with nothing of ourselves. We know it's all about Him. When we see all that God has made under the sun, taking time to examine and draw near to Him through His creation, our natural heart will respond with praise. When we consistently point our children to God and His handiwork with thankfulness, worship will follow—it's what we were created to do!

Questions to Ponder

• After spending time with God today studying His creation, think about the area toward which you feel He is calling you to be a more intentional steward.

Faith-Filled Ideas

Start a nature table and journal with your children. Begin collecting different items from nature that you find. Take note of animals and insects that you see or read about. When you discover something, have your children illustrate or write about it in an ongoing nature journal. Backyard bird feeders are a great way to bring in wildlife for you and your children to view and identify.

Find a way to care for animals. Remind your children how God cares for them and how we should too. Some simple ways God has shown me over the years are to shop humanely for food when possible and to avoid buying products needlessly tested on animals and instead purchase alternatives.

Read the creation story as a family and celebrate what God has done! Talk about how we are made in his image and the innate value that we hold as humans created for life. If your children are old enough, discuss the origin of life in the womb beginning at conception, and pray against abortion and the assault against God's creation.

journal

_____

_____

_____

_____

_____

_____

_____

_____

_____

_____

Forgiveness

"Father, forgive them,
for they do not know what they are doing."
~ Luke 23:34

Dear Sister,

We are so thankful you joined us for *The Wise Woman Loves* Bible study. We pray that you have been changed by the power of the Holy Spirit. Our final week of studies is about forgiveness. Forgiveness can be difficult, but it is so important. Some say *unforgiveness* is like drinking poison and thinking the other person will die. Unforgiveness poisons our hearts and weighs us down with bitterness.

If there is one thing Scripture is clear about, it is that we must forgive others as God forgave us (Ephesians 4:32). The following studies may challenge you, but know that we, at the Help Club for Moms, are praying for you. We pray that the Father will minister to your heart. We pray He will help you forgive those who wounded you, those who sinned against you, and those who offended you.

Jesus modeled the ultimate forgiveness when He uttered from the cross, "Father, forgive them, for they do not know what they are doing" (Luke 23:34). May we receive His forgiveness today and be willing to forgive others as He forgives us.

With Blessings and Love,
Jennifer Valdois and the Help Club For Moms Team

> **"** *If we really want to love, we must learn how to forgive.* **"**
> ~ *Mother Teresa*

Mom Tips

By: Leslie Leonard

"And whenever you stand praying, if you have anything against anyone, forgive him, that your Father in heaven may also forgive you in your trespasses." ~ Mark 11:25 (NKJV)

The Wise Woman Builds Her Spirit

- Use the "Daily Plan" sheet (found in the back of your study book) three days this week. Take time to recognize the things you are grateful for in your life. Start your day on track by listing your "6 Most Important" items for the day.

- Spend one night this week reading your Bible or a devotional book. Take time to reflect on your life and pray about what God has in store for you in the future.

The Wise Woman Loves Her Husband

- Plan a date night with your husband. Has it been a while since the two of you connected without children around? Arrange for a sitter and commit to making your marriage a priority.

- Pray John 20:23 with your husband. Ask God to open your eyes and heart to show you areas where you have been unforgiving towards your husband. Ask for help in healing your relationship and letting go of the bitterness.

The Wise Woman Loves Her Children

- Teach your children Ephesians 4:32 this week. Write it on your chalkboard or a notecard in a shared space. Talk with your children about the importance of choosing to be kind, even when it is hard. Lead by example this week and extend grace towards your children in hard situations.

- Get outside with your children. Head to a local park or even your own backyard. Let your little ones enjoy the fresh air and the company of friends and family. Invite a friend to come with you to catch up.

The Wise Woman Cares For Her Home

- Start a load of clothes in the washer during breakfast three days this week. Once the clothes are clean, move them immediately to the dryer. When dry, fold and put them away before moving on to another task in your home.

- Clean and dust all the windowsills and window treatments in your home. Clear out any cobwebs and dirt. If you have time, wash the inside of the windows as well.

> **Love never gives up, never loses faith,**
> **is always hopeful, and endures through every circumstance.**
>
> ~ 1 Corinthians 13:7 (NLT)

"Never, never, never give up."
~ Winston Churchill

- Remember to call your prayer partner today! Keep it quick, and keep praying for each other throughout the week.

- Good morning, sweet mama! This week we begin our Bible studies on the topic of Forgiveness. What an important topic. Pray and ask the Holy Spirit to speak to you as you read and to prompt you of any unforgiveness you may be holding in your heart. Ask the Lord to help you obey what He is telling you to do in response to today's Bible reading.

- Read Ephesians 4:29-31 and 1 Corinthians 13: 4-8. Let the truths of these Scriptures penetrate your heart. Write these powerful verses in your journal.

Love Always Hopes

By: Deb Weakly

My childhood was filled with sadness.

I lost my mom when I was 20 years old, which meant I had no mom to help me plan a wedding, come to my house after the birth of our babies, or call for advice about issues with the children. Thankfully, the Lord gave me my precious mother-in-love, Joan Weakly, to help me in every area of my life that my mom would have usually been there for. She has been one of my greatest role-models. I have learned much from her.

Had my mom lived, it would have been challenging to say the least. She was an alcoholic and had bouts with depression and attempts at suicide. At the time of her death, she was married to an awful man, also an alcoholic who abused her physically. Yes, our family had many problems. But, you know what? I still wish I had my mom here on this earth. I miss her greatly. She would have been 84 years old this year.

Since I am in ministry, I have the honor of counseling many different types of women—some, like me, have difficult backgrounds, and some do not. Maybe your story is like mine, and you have a mom who has big issues that make it harder for the two of you to have a close relationship. Or, maybe you had a wonderful, but not perfect, Christian mom who has been overbearing or controlling. Perhaps, you have had to put "boundaries" up to keep your mom or mother-in-law from behaving a certain way or doing something you don't like.

When I prayerfully talk to the younger women in my life, I always encourage them to do their best to love and honor their parents. The apostle Paul says it quite beautifully in Ephesians 6:2-3, which is the first commandment with a promise, "Honor your father and mother...so that it may go well with you and that you may enjoy long life on the earth."

In this verse, I do not see the added words: "If your parents are godly," or, "Unless they drink," or, "As long as they are not controlling or critical." When I read this verse, I see the heart of the apostle who is encouraging us as human beings to show honor to our parents, no matter what.

Before I go any further, I realize there are many of my dear readers who have deep wounds in their hearts caused by parents. Yes, we must be wise when dealing with parents who may be addicts or abusive people. But I also know, first-hand, the power of the Gospel of Jesus Christ and extending grace and forgiveness to our loved ones even though they don't deserve it. Isn't that what Jesus did for us? As Romans 5:8 (KJV) says, "While we were yet sinners, Christ died for us."

My asking you to do your best to love and honor your parents may feel like a tall order, but I will tell you that when you do things God's way, you will be blessed. I love the rest of this verse and how it talks about the fact that when we honor our mother's and father's, all will go well with us, and we will live a long time on this earth. This is what we all want—for life to go well and to live for a long time.

What I am prayerfully proposing is for you to ask Jesus for help in the power of the Holy Spirit to love and forgive your parents for any wounds in your heart. We all need forgiveness, and God is pretty specific about what He thinks about it. Ephesians 4:32 says to "be kind and compassionate to one another, forgiving each other, just as in Christ God forgave you."

I am also asking you to prayerfully and lovingly include them in your life. In situations with my parents and in-laws, I have always tried to put myself in their shoes. How hurt would I be if my children didn't share their kids with me or were mean and controlling? I would be devastated!

I frequently visit Matthew 7:12 (NLT), "Do to others whatever you would like them to do to you. This is the essence of all that is taught in the law and the prophets."

I have known many people who struggle with harboring unforgiveness in their hearts towards their parents or in-laws. It is never a good situation. When there is hurt or unforgiveness in your heart, it causes a rift in your heart towards the other person, but it also can affect your other relationships as well. Give your hurts to God and ask for His help to love your parents or in-laws with His love. There is a reason God tells us to forgive, keep hoping and never give up on our family. Jesus knows best and modeled this perfectly. Even though His disciples deserted Him, He still came back to them after He was resurrected and forgave them!

Pray, pray, pray!! Ask the Lord to help you to share the love of Jesus with your parents and to forgive. Ask Him to give you wisdom and help know how to cultivate a loving relationship with them and to "Do unto others as you would have do unto you."

Questions to Ponder

• Are you harboring any bitterness or unforgiveness in your heart towards anyone?

• If so, what is one thing you can do today to move toward forgiveness? Ask God for wisdom and help.

Faith-Filled Ideas

Is it awkward since you've moved away? Is it stressful when you visit their house because they are not used to your children? Keep trying. Try to keep the grandchildren connected when you go back home. It *is* worth it! Someday, you are going to be in their situation, and you are going to want your grandchildren to be close to you. Modeling a good relationship now with your family will help your children to do the same when they are grown.

Author's Note: There are great resources available at many churches across the country to help bring healing from the pain of abuse from your parents or anyone else. The books *Captivating* by Stasi Eldredge, *Freedom in Christ* by Neil T. Anderson are excellent. Restoration Ministries and Healing Journey offer excellent resources as well.

journal

Forgiveness

> **"** Then Peter came up and said to him,
> 'Lord, how often will my brother sin against me, and I forgive him?
> As many as seven times?' Jesus said to him,
> 'I do not say to you seven times, but seventy-seven times.' **"**
>
> ~ Matthew 18:21-22 (ESV)

"The man or woman who doesn't forgive has forgotten the price that Christ paid for them on the Cross."
~ John Bevere

- Invite the Holy Spirit to join you in your quiet time today. God loves you so much and wants to speak with you. As you sit, be still and listen for His quiet, gentle voice. Write down what He says to you in your journal.

Are You Holding Offense?

By: Kristi Valentine

Are you holding a fence? Famous author and speaker John Bevere made a video about holding grudges in which the main character carried a white-picket fence with him. The fence symbolized holding an "offense," the barrier that unforgiveness forms in our lives.

When we hold onto bitterness and choose not to forgive people who hurt us, we end up carrying a heavy, fence-like burden wherever we go. We are emotionally, mentally, and spiritually blocked from the people and the life God intends for us.

But many people will surely offend us many times throughout our years.

In fact, as moms, our sweet children will probably be the ones to offend us most often because they lack maturity, are not perfect, and are with us much of the time. What is a mom to do?

First, let's go to the Bible and learn what God says about forgiveness. In Matthew 6:14-15 (ESV), Jesus says, "For if you forgive others their trespasses, your heavenly Father will also forgive you, but if you do not forgive others their trespasses, neither will your Father forgive your trespasses." In Matthew 18:35, He commands us to forgive our brothers from our hearts. Finally, Mark 11:25 (ESV) says, "And whenever you stand praying, forgive, if you have anything against anyone, so that your Father also, who is in heaven, may forgive you your trespasses." Clearly, God wants us to genuinely forgive others so we may receive His bountiful forgiveness!

What was Jesus' response, perfect as He was, to being offended? In His most desperate, hurting moment, innocently dying a criminal's death on the cross, His choice was to show forgiveness by asking His Heavenly Father to forgive His executioners "for they know not what they do" (Luke 23-24 ESV). Such mercy. Such love. Such beauty. Oh God, give us the grace to respond like Jesus to those who hurt us.

Forgiveness

Especially when our children are little, they truly do not realize the results of their actions and words. Costly home décor is ruined. Siblings are wounded. Food is wasted. Sleep is disregarded. Parental guidance is ignored. If Jesus were the earthly father of our children, He would forgive, no matter the cost. We have to forgive like Jesus did. We have to forgive like God commands! Jesus obeyed God and pleased God with his responses to those who offended Him.

Are you struggling with forgiveness? Have you been offended by people in your life, including your children? Psalm 86:15 (ESV) says, "But you, oh Lord, are a God merciful and gracious, slow to anger and abounding in steadfast love and faithfulness." God is not angry with you for the unforgiveness in your heart. In fact, He is full of mercy, grace, and love for you. Come to Him and ask Him to forgive your bitterness toward others. He is faithful to forgive and cleanse you from all unrighteousness (1 John 1:9).

God, please open our hearts to see people, especially our children, the way that you do. Forgive us for our unforgiveness. And give us extravagant love and Your heart for others so that even if they hurt us, we can sincerely pray, "Father, forgive them, for they know not what they do."

Questions to Ponder

• Search your heart. Do you need to forgive your children for offending you? If so, ask God to help you genuinely and quietly work through your bitterness. He is faithful to forgive you from all unrighteousness and restore a loving, healthy relationship with your children.

• Ask yourself: Who has hurt me? Whom do I need to forgive? Let the Holy Spirit do the work in you by asking Him to help you forgive the people He brings to mind.

Faith-Filled Ideas

Commit Matthew 18:21-22 (ESV) to memory, "Then Peter came up and said to him, 'Lord, how often will my brother sin against me, and I forgive him? As many as seven times?' Jesus said to him, 'I do not say to you seven times, but seventy-seven times.'"

Remind yourself of the number "seventy-seven" every time you have to speak with your child about repeat offenses. Gently teach and truly forgive your child...again.

Create a culture of forgiveness in your family by teaching your children healthy conflict resolution skills. We have been studying good communication for years in our family, and sometimes I still have to gently ask my children to remember their options for handling conflict well. Don't give up! Keep teaching and kindly reminding. It's so important! A good resource for resolving conflict in a healthy way is: *Teaching Your Children To Be Peacemakers* by Ken Sande. You can find it on the Focus on the Family website.

Forgiveness ~ Day Two

journal

_____

_____

_____

_____

_____

_____

_____

_____

_____

_____

_____

_____

_____

_____

_____

_____

_____

_____

_____

_____

_____

_____

_____

_____

_____

_____

_____

Forgiveness

> Look after each other so that none of you fails to receive the grace of God. Watch out that no poisonous root of bitterness grows up to trouble you, corrupting many.
>
> ~ Hebrews 12:15 (NLT)

"The day that Jesus was crushed for our sins, He revealed the true meaning of justice was no longer found in revenge, but in forgiveness."
~ Kris Vallotton

- Find a place where you can be alone with Jesus and your Bible. To decompress, I like to set up an environment that relaxes me (light a candle, put on light music, or open a window). Read Hebrews 12:5-15.

- Write down Hebrews 12:15 in your journal or where you will see it during your day.

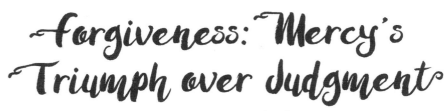

Forgiveness: Mercy's Triumph over Judgment

By: Brynne Gluch

I stood on the shoreline with my heart completely exposed. Holding the weight of my burdens and feeling humbled by the expanse of the ocean before me, I waded out knee-high into the water. As a wave approached, these words unexpectedly tumbled out of my mouth, "I forgive this betrayal, and I thank you, Lord, that you have never betrayed me." The baptismal waves crashed over my feet, overwhelming me with a newfound glimpse of freedom, washing my pain out to sea.

Ok, now let me back up and explain. I recently had the privilege to participate in a day-long workshop led by a powerhouse woman named Renee. We started the day early, coffee in hand, on the beach near my home in Coronado, California. She gave me a pebble and instructed me to put it in my shoe, take a long walk, and ask God to reveal tolerated annoyances in my life. As I walked, I was able to identify the constant, dulling pain of bitterness.

Freshly aware of my desperation for God, we headed up the road to hike Torrey Pines State Natural Reserve, which is a breathtaking place for self-reflection. After we found a bench to sit on, we processed what causes bitterness to take root. My answer was self-protection. I realized that although the boundaries I set with unrepentant people are healthy, I also use these boundaries to justify disconnection. I had been failing to trust God with judgment and preventing His Spirit from tending to the brokenness of my heart.

As we headed down the trail toward the water, she had me list offenses I've held. As one would come to mind, I would share, and she would pick up a rock to put in my backpack. It became heavy, as did my heart. We talked about how my relationships felt strained because my heart had become too tender and could no longer preserve intimacy in the face of conflict.

So, there at the shore, I unloaded my rocks into the sea. A different word seemed to come from deep within me to describe each injustice stone. I'd say, "I forgive this misunderstanding, and I thank you, Lord, that you have never misunderstood me." Then I'd say, "I forgive this accusation. Thank you, Father, for defeating the accuser." And so on. The truth was renewing my mind. God was who I needed Him to be each time others had fallen short of my needs and expectations. I could feel my heart start to open, resentment softening into restoration.

After I had thrown out the last rock, Renee came over and handed me another stone. This one was not jagged as the others had been, but smooth. She put it in my hand and said, "Now, go forgive yourself." Somehow, this seemed the hardest to do. But God spoke to me through the smoothness of the stone—that it was His mercy to refine me, but against his character to punish me in judgment. With that, I released my final stone, and His grace consumed my shame.

We ended the workshop with communion. As I received the elements of bread and wine, I recognized that it is through my undeserved forgiveness that I can find peace leaving justice in the hands of a good God.

Questions to Ponder

• What does Scripture say about forgiveness? (Mark 11:26)

• How did Jesus treat those who wronged Him? (Luke 23:34)

• What does clinical psychology say about the physical effects of unforgiveness? Learn more at https://www.hopkinsmedicine.org/health/healthy_aging/healthy_connections/forgiveness-your-health-depends-on-it.

• What is forgiveness *not*? (Psalm 55:22, i.e. approval of wrongdoing, exemption for prosecution of illegal action, requirement of reconciliation with an abuser)

Faith-Filled Ideas

Spend a day with the Lord with the intention of self-care. Go for a hike with a sack of injustice rocks. Unload your burdens to the Lord. I know it can be hard to get away, but remember the airplane metaphor: we must put our own oxygen masks on before we can help our families. Here are a few things to keep in mind on your journey:

Give yourself loads of grace in this process. This is hard soul-work! But when I am unkind to myself or others, the Holy Spirit is not present in that judgment. We need to let shame go and allow Him to woo us with His love, patience, joy, intentionality, faithfulness, and goodness.

Forgiveness sets us FREE. Hebrews 12 challenges us to press into the discipline of the Lord, which feels painful at the moment but produces a peaceful harvest in our lives. Forgiving can feel like an obligation, but as the Lord lifts burdens, that feeling will turn to liberation. "Letting it go" is a spiritual practice of trust.

Let the Spirit lead you! If God prompts a desire to restore a particular broken relationship during your time with Him, you may need to have a love-filled conversation and mend it. Ask Him for divine strategy.

Journal. Write down your experience for the next time you need to forgive because there is power in testimonies of God's victory!

Pursue More. If you would like more information on the workshop, you can contact Renee at donandrenee.com.

journal

Forgiveness ~ Day Three

Forgiveness

Forgiveness is the theme for the week. Forgiveness of any sort requires one to be humble. When I think of humility, the Proverbs 31 woman comes to mind. She is a woman of noble character. She sets about her work vigorously, and her arms are strong for the task. She is clothed in strength and dignity. She speaks with wisdom, and faithful instruction is on her tongue. She watches over the affairs of her household and does not eat the bread of idleness. Her children rise and call her blessed, and her husband also. Many women do noble things, but she surpasses them all.

These are just a few descriptions of the Proverbs 31 woman. Doesn't she sound like a humble woman who easily forgives? I was trying to think of a recipe that could represent the Proverbs 31 woman, and humble chicken and rice soup is just perfect. When you try this recipe, try to channel your inner Proverbs 31 woman. Be inspired and encouraged by all you do for your home and family.

HUMBLE AND HEARTY CHICKEN AND RICE SOUP

By: Brandi Carson and Meagan Witt

Ingredients:

2 pounds chicken drumsticks

½ cup of rice

4 celery stalks, chopped

½ an onion, chopped

4 garlic cloves, minced

4 carrots, chopped

1 Jalapeño, chopped *optional

Directions:

1. Place drumsticks, water, salt, and pepper in a dutch oven on medium heat. Bring to a boil. Boil for 20 minutes.

2. Chop veggies. Add rice and veggies to the dutch oven. Cook for an additional 20 minutes.

3. Remove drumsticks from the pot. Shred the chicken off the bone, then add the shredded chicken back to the pot. Stir.

4. Serve and enjoy!

Anger Toolbox!

for Kids

By: Tara Davis

Some days it seems as if the roar of kid frustration or sibling squabbles is the perpetual soundtrack of motherhood, doesn't it? It can be so exhausting and can weigh heavily on our hearts, but God provides all we need to help our kids. When we give them an internal toolbox filled with strategies to deal with anger and frustration, we are providing them with a gift they will carry their whole lives through.

The pursuit of filling your children's toolbox is a worthy one, sweet friends! The activity below will prompt your kiddos to begin learning methods that will help them each and every day.

DIRECTIONS:

1. **PRAY** — "Before we begin this activity, let's pray together and ask the Lord to give us wisdom to help us work through frustrations in ways that shine the love of Jesus."

2. **STORY** — Read the story on page 182 aloud to your child.

3. **BUILD & DISCUSS** — Help your child manage their anger in an appropriate way with this fun toolbox! Simply make a toolbox out of two pieces of paper stapled on top of one another to form a pocket, cut the tools out, and let your child color as you talk about ways to deal with frustration that are pleasing to the Lord and encouraging to others! "Now, we will look at some tools to help us as we face problems in life."

4. **CONCLUSION** — "After we build our toolboxes, let's talk about how Sara could have handled her frustration differently and how you can handle daily frustrations differently too. And remember, God loves you so much regardless of how you are feeling, and I do too!"

The Anger TOOLBOX

In your anger, do not sin.
Ephesians 4:26

STORY: Sara awoke early on a Saturday morning, the brilliant sun filtering through her curtains and scattering speckles of light across her bedroom floor. "This is going to be the best day ever!" she thought as she slipped on her clothes and hurried down for breakfast. There was a big art project waiting on the kitchen table that she had begun the night before. She had made a sculpture out of clay for her friend's birthday present, and today she was going to paint it.

Just then, a loud BANG! erupted from the direction of the kitchen. Oh no, her art project! Sara ran into the kitchen just in time to see her beautiful clay sculpture and paints crashing to the floor. Her sculpture had broken into pieces and the pots of paint had spilled all over the kitchen tile. Oh, how her heart ached! "How did this happen?" she wondered aloud. As she glanced up, she noticed her little brother shrinking back into a corner of the kitchen, a shadow of sadness crossing his face. "How could you?!" she yelled.

He tried to explain that it was an accident and that he had only meant to look at her project, but her heart was racing too fast to listen. She yelled at him and said things that she knew were wrong as she stormed back to her bedroom, slamming the door behind her. "I am so mad!" she cried as she considered ways she could get even with her brother.

After a few minutes, she opened her door and walked decidedly toward his room and his newly built Lego set displayed neatly on his dresser. Quickly, Sara picked up the set and threw it to the floor. As her brother's creation shattered into tiny pieces, she only felt worse. How her anger had gotten the best of her! If only she had made things go differently, she thought as fresh tears stung her eyes and her heart sank.

Have you ever had an experience like Sara in which you felt so angry that you had a hard time controlling your actions and your words? We all have, but the amazing thing is that God has given us tools, both in His Word and through the Holy Spirit, to help us solve our problems. We do not have to let anger and frustration rule our words and actions. We can walk with Jesus through each problem we face; He will help us every day!

Anger
Tool Box

Let the peace of Christ rule in
your hearts. Colossians 3:15

PRAY and cast your
cares on the Lord

CONSTRUCTION MANUAL:
BIBLE
READ God's
Word and
follow it

Find a different
ACTIVITY (run, climb a tree,
make something)

Take a
BREAK to
help you
calm down

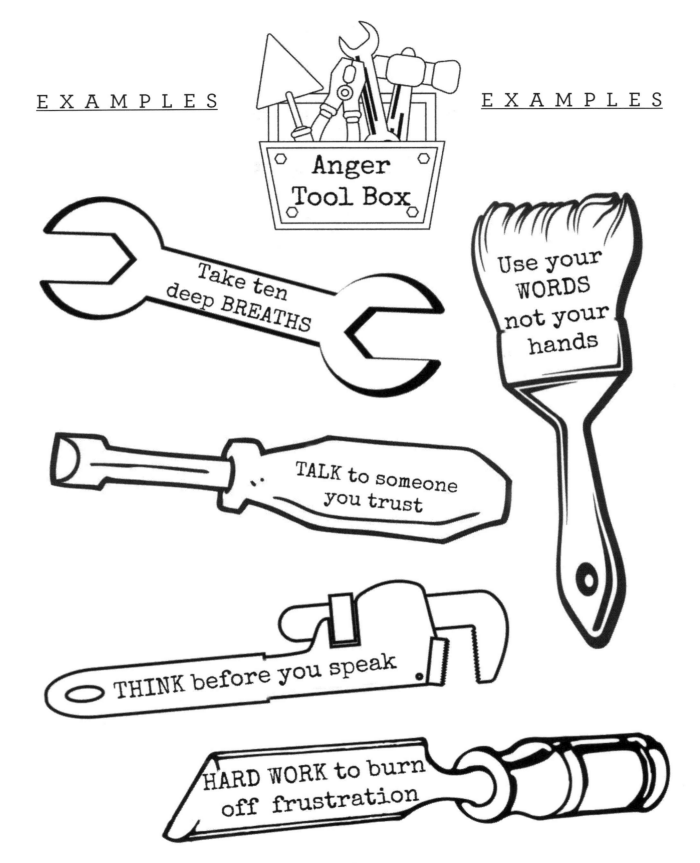

Anger Tool Box

Take ten deep BREATHS

Use your WORDS not your hands

TALK to someone you trust

THINK before you speak

HARD WORK to burn off frustration

My ----→ **TOOLBOX**

Cut Tools and Color!

"Let's take a moment to pray and ask God for which tools He wants us to use when we feel angry!"

Customize your own tools!

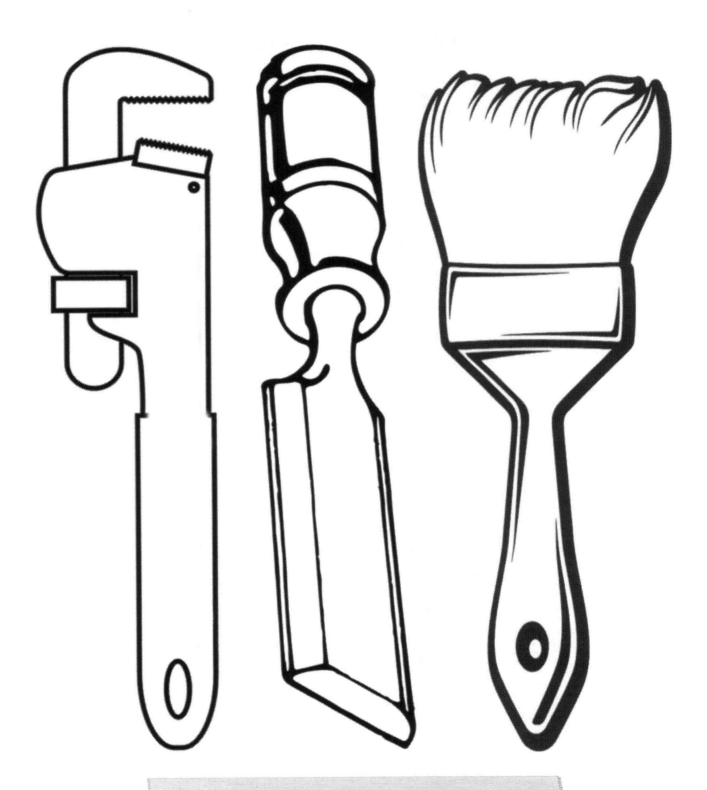

Customize your own tools!

Help Club For Moms is a community of moms who encourage one another to know the love of Jesus. Our ministry cultivates mom-to-mom relationships through online social media platforms, and our small group and church programs. We believe prayer changes everything and God is big enough to help us raise our children in today's culture. We focus on digging into God's Word, praying together, and seeking to become the women, wives, and mothers God created us to be.

We inspire women through practical Bible study devotionals, "Mom Tips," "Faith-Filled Ideas," and kid's discipleship tools to help nurture joy-filled homes overflowing with the love of Jesus.

Would you like to be a part of the movement?

Here's how you can get involved in the Help Club for Moms:

- *The Wise Woman Builds, The Wise Woman Cares, The Wise Woman Enjoys,* and *The Wise Woman Knows* by Help Club For Moms are available on Amazon.

- Pray for the ministry and the moms in our Help Club Community worldwide—for them to know the love of Jesus and create a Christ-like atmosphere in their homes.

- Start a Help Club for Moms group at your local church or home. We can help you!

- We are always on the lookout for Titus 2 women who can help mentor our moms through social media and prayer.

- If you are an author, blogger, graphics artist, or social media guru, we need you and your talents at the Help Club!

- **Donate.** We are a 501(c)(3) and all-volunteer ministry! Please go to **helpclubformoms.com/donate/** to help us reach moms all around the world.

You can find out more about Help Club for Moms at helpclubformoms.com and on Facebook and Instagram @HelpClubForMoms.

WANT TO START A
"HELP CLUB FOR MOMS" GROUP
AT YOUR CHURCH?

CONTACT INFO@HELPCLUBFORMOMS.COM!

Church Resource Section

Moms encouraging moms to know the love of Christ

Dear Mom,

We are so very honored that you are journeying through this Bible study with us. What a gift you are to our ministry!

We wanted to make sure you knew that, built right into this book, is everything you need to start a "Help Club for Moms" group of your own! You can do it through your church or even as a small group in your home. Lives are changed when we read God's Word together and focus on becoming intentional moms and wives in community together! Doing a Help Club for Moms Bible Study is a chance for you and your friends to dive deeper into learning about God's design for motherhood. Plus, everything is more fun with friends!

It is so easy to lead a Help Club for Moms group. Each mom commits to following along in the Bible study. Then you meet at your home or church just twice per month to go over what you are learning and pray for one another. We even have a special group on Facebook dedicated to our Help Club for Moms Bible Study Leaders where we give you ideas with lesson plans for your group. Simply go to the *Help Club for Moms National Leaders Group* on Facebook, answer the questions and ask to join. It's that simple!

Doing life together as moms in a Christ-centered community draws us closer to Jesus and to each other while building friendship and connections that are sure to last a lifetime. What a great way to walk as moms, together arm-in-arm and with our eyes on Jesus, all the way until we get to heaven.

If you are interested in starting a Help Club for Moms group, either in your church or home, please email us at info@helpclubformoms.com. We would love to walk alongside you, give you helpful resources, and PRAY for you.

Blessings to you, mama!

Sincerely,

The Help Club for Moms Team

FAQ:
About Help Club For Moms

WHAT IS THE HELP CLUB FOR MOMS?

• Help Club for Moms is a community of moms encouraging moms to know the love of Christ. We value authentic, transparent relationships. Together, we study God's Word, pray, fellowship twice a month, and share practical "Mom Tips." All this to become the women, wives, and mothers God created us to be, and with the help of the Holy Spirit, bring up our children to do the same!

WHY CHOOSE HELP CLUB?

• Help Club For Moms offers a Christ-centered program focused on strengthening the church by strengthening moms, through teaching God's design for families and biblically based parenting.

• There is no fee for the program; the only cost is for the books which may be purchased on Amazon.

• The program is for moms of all ages. We love learning from each other in every stage of life!

• There are three simple, but deep, biblical studies per week, which teach and encourage moms, yet are still easy to accomplish. A must for today's busy mom!

• Help Club For Moms "Mom Tips" set us apart from other mom groups because every week, we offer eight practical, new ideas to strengthen and train women in their role as a wife, mother, and woman of God.

• Each mom in Help Club For Moms is partnered with another mom for prayer. Every week, these two moms pray for 10-15 minutes with one another over the phone, deepening their connection with God and each other. Prayer changes everything!

• Help Club For Moms brings godly community, support, fellowship, and friendship to families through the relationships formed between moms.

• HCFM's has three years of Christ-centered curriculum.

• HCFM has a strong presence on social media, which helps moms go deeper in the studies with other moms around the world.

WHAT ARE THE CORE VALUES OF HELP CLUB FOR MOMS?

• HCFM values authentic and transparent community between moms, deep growth in relationship with God, intentional Bible study, faithful prayer relationships between moms, and practical day-to-day ideas and tips for moms.

WHAT IS REQUIRED OF THE CHURCH?

• HCFM's partner churches should plan to help in two ways:
  1. Offer a meeting space for two hours/twice monthly
  2. Help with childcare for two hours/twice monthly

Hosting a HCFM's Meeting

WHAT DOES A TYPICAL HELP CLUB FOR MOMS MEETING LOOK LIKE?

• Hosting a Help Club meeting is easy and fun and is a great way to build community with the moms in your church or neighborhood. Below is a sample morning meeting schedule. (You could also host a "Help Club Mom's Night Out Potluck Dinner" instead of a daytime meeting for working moms or moms who want some time away while dad has the children.)

SCHEDULE

9:30-9:40 **Welcome, pray, and on time drawing with an inexpensive prize**

9:40-10:15 **Moms meet in groups to discuss current HCFM Bible study**
- Large groups: Moms sit around tables in small groups of 3-6 moms with a leader and possible co-leader to discuss content from the last two week's topic.
- Small groups or home study group: Moms sit in a circle as one big group to discuss content from the last two week's topic.

10:15-10:30 **Simple worship and announcements** (HCFM Spotify and Amazon Prime playlist and lyrics provided if desired)

10:30-10:35 **Book Review** (HCFM suggested book review provided if desired)

10:35-10:50 **Mom Tips in Action** (Invite one of your leaders/ helpers to spotlight a Mom Tip from this week's study and how she used it) Then, invite other moms from the group to share how they used a moms tip from the list or how they are planning to use one in the future. This is an important time for our moms to learn from each other.

10:50-11:15 **Devotion time**
There are two ways to facilitate a HCFM's devotion portion of the group: one led by a seasoned mom or one led by a young, peer aged mom.
- Both groups lead a discussion about the topic from the last two weeks of study by discussing Scripture and asking questions of the group about the topic. (Scripture applicable to the topic and "Questions to Ponder" are found in each study.) The leader shares her personal experiences as a fellow mom journeying on the road of motherhood. The leader may also choose to watch a portion of a Help Club for Moms "Mentoring Monday" video about the topic with the moms in her group.

11:15-11:25 **Moms pray with prayer partners**

11:25 **Pray and dismiss moms to pick up children**

All HCFM leaders have access to a private Facebook group (Help Club for Moms National Group Leaders) where they can access training videos, ask questions, and share ideas to help them host a successful group. **Questions? Email us at info@helpclubformoms.com.**

Book Recommendations

BOOKS FOR MOMS (NON-FICTION):

Parenting the Wholehearted Child
  by Jeannie Cunnion

You and Me Forever by Francis and Lisa Chan
  (marriage)

Daring Greatly by Brene Brown

The Ragamuffin Gospel by Brennan Manning

Love and Respect by Dr. Emmerson Eggerichs

Love and Respect in the family
  by Dr. Emmerson Eggerichs

Mother and Son by Dr. Emmerson Eggerichs

The Circle Maker by Mark Batterson

The Power of a Praying Wife
  by Stormie O' Martian

The Power of a Praying Parent
  by Stormie O' Martian

The Read-Aloud Family by Sarah Mackenzie

BOOKS FOR MOMS (FICTION):

Mark of the Lion trilogy by Francine Rivers

Redeeming Love by Francine Rivers

Sarah's Key by Tatiana de Rosnay

The Help by Kathryn Stockett

BOOKS FOR KIDS:

Discipleship books:

The Picture Bible published by David C. Cook

The Jesus Storybook Bible by Sally Lloyd-Jones

The Action Bible by Sergio Cariello

Missionary Stories with the Millers
  by Mildred A. Martin

Upper Elementary/Early Middle School (grades 4-7):

The Wingfeather Saga by Andrew Peterson

The Green Ember series by E.D. Smith

The Penderwicks series by Jeanne Birdsall

Lower Elementary (grades 2-3):

The Imagination Station by Marianne Hering

Greetings from Somewhere by Harper Paris

Dear Molly, Dear Olive by Megan Atwood

Early Readers (grades K-1):

Owl Diaries by Rebecca Elliot

I Can Read! Princess Parables by Jeanna Young

Jotham's Journey series

Little House on the Prairie by Laura Ingalls Wilder

The BFG by Roald Dahl

The Lion, The Witch, and the Wardrobe
  by C.S. Lewis

Anne of Green Gables by Lucy Maud Montgomery

HOMESCHOOLING:

Teaching From Rest by Sarah Mackenzie

Educating the WholeHearted Child
  by Clay Clarkson with Sally Clarkson

Seasons of a Mother's Heart by Sally Clarkson

Podcasts

PODCASTS FOR MOMS:

Don't Mom Alone

Coffee & Crumbs

Java with Juli

Cultivating the Lovely

Parenting Great Kids with Dr. Meg Meeker

Focus on the Family

The Messenger Podcast

Conversations with John and Lisa Bevere

I am Adamant Podcast by Lisa Bevere

Read Aloud Revival

Happy Hour with Jamie Ivey

PODCASTS FOR KIDS:

Stories Podcast

Storynory

Brains On! Science Podcast for Kids

Adventures in Odyssey

ONLINE SERMONS:

ChurchoftheHighlands.org

Theaterchurch.org

Worship Music

PANDORA HELP CLUB FOR MOMS STATION:

https://pdora.co/2KynyvV

SPOTIFY HELP CLUB FOR MOMS STATION:

https://spoti.fi/2lVBMbw

Made in the USA
Monee, IL
08 January 2020